Believe in You
You are triumphant.
You are Victorious!
With love, ♥
Victoria

# Victorious

## A Woman's Journey of Survival, Transformation, and Healing

**VICTORIA JONES GRIFFITH**

ISBN: 978-1-54395-191-2 (print)

ISBN: 978-1-54395-192-9 (ebook)

## Disclaimer

The events portrayed in this book are correct to the best of my memory. While this is a work of nonfiction and all the stories in this book are true, some names and other details have been altered to protect the privacy of those involved.

## Dedication

The day that I decided that my book was finally finished and ready to be published, my 11-year-old chihuahua Pepe decided that it was time to leave this Earth. Pepe came to me during the darkest time in my life. He licked my tears and made me laugh. As you will see in my book, his assignment was clear. So, I dedicate this book to Pepe, one of my guardian angels who has taught me what unconditional love truly is.

# ACKNOWLEDGMENTS

Upon feeling a nudge from God, I began writing my story on August 16, 2017 which was exactly two months before the "Me Too" movement began. First, I would like to acknowledge, all the women who have found their voice, who are in the process of discovering their voice, and those who will find theirs after reading my story.

I want to thank:

Amy Wienecke, Developmental Editor and Writing Coach, for her remarkable gift of editing and coaching, for encouraging me and inspiring me to dig deeper, and for her unwavering belief in me throughout my writing journey.

Jheni Solis, Copy Editor and fellow "One Billion Rising" Lead Dance Instructor, for giving my manuscript the final read before sending it into the world.

Marjorie for our "chicken soup for the soul" conversations about healing and for being the first one to read my manuscript.

Amy S., Atoosa, Cherry, Cindy, Elizabeth, Holly, Janet, Jen, Karen, Kim, Linda, Meissa, Nancy, Quitman, and Will —who believed in me and cheered me on along the way.

My twin sister Mandy for her unconditional love and unwavering support throughout my healing and writing process.

My parents for allowing me to move towards my pain so that I could discover my power: My mother for being a constant beacon of light and positivity (and the inspiration behind my cover design), and my father for instilling in me the principles of character and service.

# CONTENTS

INTRODUCTION ............................................................... xi

## THE VICTIM

CHAPTER 1 -   Ignorance is Bliss ................................... 2
CHAPTER 2 -   "V" For Victim ....................................... 9
CHAPTER 3 -   Perfectly Imperfect ...............................21

## THE VALIDATION

CHAPTER 4 -   Numbing the Pain ................................. 30
CHAPTER 5 -   Prey Not Pray ....................................... 37
CHAPTER 6 -   50 Shades of Terrible ............................ 44
CHAPTER 7 -   Sweaty Money ...................................... 54

## THE VOICE

CHAPTER 8 -   Ascending the Mountain ..................... 66
CHAPTER 9  -  I Found My Guru ................................. 70
CHAPTER 10 - The Dark Night of the Soul ................. 78
CHAPTER 11 - Bait and Switch ................................... 83
CHAPTER 12 - Rise Up ............................................... 91
CHAPTER 13 - Fight, Flight, or Freeze and Why I Didn't Report. 95
CHAPTER 14 - The Gym Manager, The Pastor, & The Producer . 101

## THE VULNERABILITY

CHAPTER 15 - My Millennial Meltdown .................... 110

## THE VICTORY

CHAPTER 16 - The Victory Dance ............................. 118
CHAPTER 17 - Ok, So Now What? ............................ 122

Stone carving of the Greek goddess Nike, the goddess of victory, which is her Roman equivalent to Victoria, at the ruins of the ancient city of Ephesus.

# INTRODUCTION

"Only when we are brave enough to
explore the darkness will we discover
the infinite power of the light."

- Brené Brown

Vic-to-ri-ous: having won a victory; triumphant

It was 2007 and an unusually cold December in Texas. I remember opening my eyes to complete pitch black darkness and shivering uncontrollably. A sudden flood of thoughts started racing through my head. Was I dreaming? Was I dead? Had I been kidnapped? All I was sure of at that moment was the feeling of hard, freezing concrete beneath my naked body. I somehow gathered the strength to crawl towards what appeared to be a small sliver of light in the distance. I located what felt like a door, and I pushed it open. And there I was — naked, cold, and alone in the morning light. As the light spilled over me, I knew this was it. I could no longer be a victim.

The younger of identical twins by seventeen minutes, my parents named me Victoria. A few years ago, my mother took a trip to Greece, bringing me an unusual souvenir — a photograph she took of a stone carving of the Greek goddess Nike. This was particularly special because I discovered, after brushing up on my history, that the Romans gave this goddess a name too: goddess Victoria, the goddess of victory. This keepsake became one of my mental anchors, helping me focus on my own personal victory when things got tough. Victory over the need for perfection and self-defeat. Victory over self-sabotage and shame. Victory armed with self-love, self-worth, and self-respect.

This is not a story of traditional abuse and sexual assault that you so often see on the evening news or in your social media feed. My story is an even more common one. It is the kind of story that hides in the shadow of fear and shame and is not often openly addressed by our society. Unlike recovering from external wounds from a tragic accident, fall or other bodily injuries, these wounds are on the inside, and most carry them for a lifetime. Many women are afraid that if they tell their story, they won't be believed. So they never heal, often becoming perpetual victims.

Even before my first assault, I suffered from a lack of self-love and self-respect. I suffered from the inability to establish personal boundaries, as well as my overwhelming need for perfection. I didn't realize at the time that these things were the root of every violation I would experience over the next 22 years of my life.

As I began to write my story, I struggled with mentioning divinity, not because I wanted to appeal to the masses, but because of my own personal experience with God and church. When I was at my lowest, caught in a cycle of self-loathing, shame and guilt, I thought I had disappointed God and that He was punishing me for my choices. Like Hester Prynne in the famous novel, The Scarlet Letter, I had branded myself with my own invisible scarlet letter "V", convinced that I would always be a victim; so I did not want to hear about God, the God I knew as an innocent young girl. I felt anyone talking about Him, quoting scripture, and going to church, hadn't experienced the same pain I was going through. This was a lie I was telling myself. Whether you believe in God, Creator, Universe, or a Higher Power, I pray that my story helps you grow stronger in your faith: a faith in something much bigger than yourself and a faith that will lead you out of any personal darkness.

Part of my story involves my work over the past 20 years as a Certified Health and Wellness Expert. I discovered that my clients were following my customized workouts and diet plans, but they weren't keeping the weight off. I had to look at why I was still having digestive issues and holding on to excess weight if I was following my own plan perfectly. After years of searching for answers to heal myself, I discovered that the most important workout was the workout that begins inside all of us. Our divine DNA is meant to thrive. I genuinely believe that a great deal of our "diseases" (dis-ease, unease) such as weight gain, extreme weight loss, depression, chronic fatigue, physical pain, and our inability to heal come from holding onto past wounds and fears. And after personally letting go of my pain, my shame, and my fear little by little, I saw a stronger woman emerge. On the inside, I became healthier, more energized, joyful, and optimistic. On the outside, my belly became flatter, my digestive issues went away, and I began to look leaner and more youthful. People began asking me what I was doing differently. I was working out less than I ever had in the past and was not even as strict on my diet. This was an INSIDE job. I began to use these techniques I discovered with my clients, and I was amazed to see how they too began to transform on the outside.

I spent many years not only angry at the men who hurt me but blaming myself for being a victim and not having the courage to report my assaults. I didn't have a support network or a roadmap to follow to help me feel whole again. Many times, I have wished I could go back and talk to the younger me. Tell her to talk to someone. Tell her it isn't her fault. Tell her that she's loved and important. Tell her she has worth and value.

My intention in writing this book is not to shame those who hurt me, disrupt their lives and families in any way, or to lay fault or blame even on myself. I have changed all the names and have told my truth through the lens of love, compassion, and forgiveness. One of my biggest blessings (and my greatest curse) is that I always see the best in everyone I meet. That is part of the reason why I stayed with some of these men for so long. I truly believe that these men, and all humans, can change and evolve like I have.

This is the story of my journey, my transformation from a victim to a victor. It's a journey that occurred in stages: a naive girl with strong religious conviction struggling physically to maintain her "perfect" outer appearance; a young woman struggling mentally with believing that she is damaged goods after breaking what she thought was her pact with God; an adult woman struggling emotionally and seeking emotional stability while searching for love in all the wrong places; and a woman who found the love she was searching for her entire life.

Today, I am ready to speak my truth and share my story so that other women like me will know they are not alone and can receive the tools I used to heal my wounds, fall in love with myself and live a victorious life.

# THE VICTIM

# CHAPTER 1

# Ignorance is Bliss

"Love is what we were born with.
Fear is what we learned here."

- Marianne Williamson

I grew up in the 1980s and early 1990s in the highly sought-after Highland Park, a city within a city, in the middle of Dallas, Texas. It is often referred to as "the Bubble" by many because it seems like a perfect, protected, utopian area that is exempt from the typical modern problems of a big city. My family was the picture of the typical conservative and happy family.

Middle school is tough for most kids, but for me, it was particularly difficult. It was when I was introduced to my so-called friends — shame, humiliation, and fear. I was not one of the kids that had a growth spurt and sprouted up, but rather one that sprouted "out." Holding onto baby fat was especially difficult when you live in a "perfect" little bubble community. I was not able to fit into any of my own clothes, so my mother gave me one of her black knit skirts to wear to school because it had an extra stretchy elastic waistband. Already a self-conscious 12-year-old girl, this amplified my insecurities.

I managed to make it through the school day and was headed out of the school doors to begin my usual walk home when two boys, who frequently made fun of me and called me names, came up from behind yelling, "Something's going down!" I ignored them and kept walking toward the edge of campus until there it was again, "Something's going down!" And then I realized what was going down — my borrowed black stretchy knit skirt, down around my ankles. Tears burst out of my eyes and onto my cheeks. I pulled up my skirt as fast as I could and began a fast sprint toward my house which seemed like another continent away. I arrived sobbing, trembling, and feeling humiliated. I ran to my mother and told her I was never going back to school again. She told me that she was going to call both boys' mothers, and I begged her not to. I knew if she did, those boys would make my life worse. That was the first time I lost my voice. It was more important to fit in than speak up... something I would become very familiar with.

My first experience with love was through the extraordinary bond I had with my identical twin sister. We were inseparable. We began singing together in school musicals, dancing on the drill team together, dating a few of the same boys, and sharing a wardrobe. We even got voted "Best Couple" on our high school Senior Poll. Although we were identical twins and obviously as close as two people could be, I always felt different. This feeling of difference extended to the rest of my family as well for some reason, and I couldn't pinpoint it. I felt I was forcing myself to fit in and always do the right thing. My quest for perfection began.

This need to be perfect carried over to all aspects of my life. Church was everything to me. I went to weekly Bible studies, church camp every summer, and religious retreats at every opportunity. I initially was introduced to church by one of my first boyfriends. Derek had very strict religious practices that were in stark contrast to typically expected high-school behaviors like experimenting with alcohol and physical contact with the opposite sex. He considered these behaviors to be monumental sins, sending daily Bible verses to remind me we shouldn't even lay on top of each other and why it was so wrong. This made such a lasting impression on me that I made a vow to myself that I would save myself for marriage.

Derek wasn't the only one with these stringent religious beliefs and practices at our school. There was a small group of both girls and guys with the same views, and we bonded together in our own clique. Labeled by our peers as the "Bible Bangers," we were often ostracized and alienated by the other kids. My extreme adherence to my beliefs resulted in a lack of invitations to parties and even more exclusion because I made others uncomfortable; so I focused all of my time and energy into my studies and dance.

I was not a natural student and often struggled in school. My twin inherited the gift of being able to take a test and ace it without even studying. In contrast, I had to bury my nose in my books for days to keep up. However, the hard work paid off, and I ended up graduating at the top of my class with honors. The perfectionist in me wouldn't have had it any other way, but dancing was more my thing.

I started dancing tap at the age of five, and I remember the ease and excitement I experienced. I finally felt like I was a part of something bigger and no longer isolated and different from everyone else. I finally felt free, with a way to express myself when I was dancing. Dancing became my escape from the many other boundaries ruling every other aspect of my life. I tried out for drill team my freshman year and made it. Dancing gave me so much confidence. I even made lieutenant my junior year, which is a year earlier than most; but that was when my need to be perfect was challenged. We had very strict weight and measurement requirements on drill team, and in my junior year, I struggled to meet those requirements. I remember how it felt to be measured with that cold measuring tape and my thighs being over the number they were supposed to be on the health chart. I had to sit out on the sidelines because of my "thunder thighs." This was the first time I felt like I was a failure. I had disappointed my squad, my team, my family, and myself. I felt shame for the second time in my life.

As a result, I don't use measurements as my criteria of success for my wellness coaching clients to this day. I now realize using those measurements was a very archaic, "one-size-fits-all" method, a method that proved to be quite damaging to young teenage girls who were already insecure about their bodies.

My obsession with my weight and physical appearance began with those drill team practices. I felt a need for complete control over another aspect of my life; this time with food and exercise. I never wanted to feel that shame of being forced to sit out again, so I started to starve myself and over-exercise. I would exercise up to two hours a day, in addition to the workouts required by the drill team. That did the trick, and the weight came off. My thigh measurements went down, I felt I was part of the group again, and most importantly, I got the opportunity to dance again. Unfortunately, no one could have known the pain that was growing inside of me.

I made it to my senior year and from the outside looking in, I had conquered it all. I was a second-year lieutenant of an award-winning drill team, student council representative, nominated for homecoming court, dating one of the star players on our football team and making straight A's. However, everything was not as it seemed. I had managed to become even thinner by pretending to eat and bragging to everyone how much I ate as a distraction. I knew I wasn't fooling my parents; I was only fooling myself. I didn't care; I was happy with my personal sense of control. I was "perfect."

Before I knew it, it was time to choose a college, because that's what everyone did who graduated from my high school. I narrowed it down to the University of Texas. I had my own dorm room and even auditioned for the dance department. My father, who is the epitome of "Mr. UT," was thrilled. Though everything seemed to be lining up perfectly, the stage was set for my very first heartbreak. One of my girlfriends invited me to a college party in Fort Worth on the Texas Christian University campus, and I decided to go. I had not even considered TCU when narrowing down colleges because it was too close to home, and I yearned to escape the bubble I was living in.

When I showed up to meet my friend, she told me she had arranged dates for us with a couple of fraternity boys to accompany us to the party. The thought of going to a fraternity party was frightening enough, but the prospect of having a date as well made me sweaty and nervous. I was innocent, naive and comfortably rooted in my no drinking/no smoking/no sex bubble version of high school and church life. I was terrified.

I found the courage to attend the party and found myself enjoying my date's company despite his persistence that I should "live a little" and drink with everyone. I managed to stay my strong "perfect" self and successfully avoided all of my date's attempts to make me drink. Strangely enough, I decided I might like this guy. We didn't have much in common, but there was something about him, and I had never had feelings like this. A thousand butterflies flying around in my stomach was a feeling hard to ignore.

Looking back, I realize this was mistake number one of many I would make with men. This one party was instrumental in changing my direction. I decided the next day I was no longer going to the University of Texas and instead applied to Texas Christian University. My parents were shocked, but still happy because I had chosen a school that my paternal grandmother attended. What they did not know and would not have been happy about was that I was basing my decision on the new boy in my life, William. It was a big decision for a boy I knew very little about.

# CHAPTER 2

# "V" For Victim

"You have been branded with many labels in
your life. Some you wear like a badge, some
like a medal, and some you wear shamefully
like "The Scarlett Letter." Regardless, not
a single one of them defines you."

- Author Unknown

The "Freshman 15," a term that refers to weight often gained by students their first year in college (and largely attributed to copious amounts of pizza and beer), skipped me entirely. Instead, I lost weight. It was 1992 as I began my freshman year at TCU, and I was ready to start my new life with my own identity, separate from my identical twin sister. Instead of one of "The Griffith Twins," I was Vickie, short for Victoria, (my given name which held so much symbolism). What I didn't realize at the time was how this separation from my twin sister would be one of the most difficult losses I would ever experience. I no longer had the backup I was used to, which eventually forced me to grow and become stronger. Today, though we have both gone very different directions in life, we are still very close.

I dove in head first and went through sorority rush because that is what everybody did from Highland Park and it was expected. William, the boy I was still crazy about, was now an impressive sophomore and advised me on which sorority I should join. I took his advice and joined a sorority. It wasn't long until I realized that the perfect, strong, independent girl from high school was not as strong as she thought she was.

William invited me to his fraternity Victory Party, a pledge celebration thrown by each of the fraternities and sororities, and I agreed to go. I found it more important to do what he wanted than attend my own Victory Party to celebrate with my new sorority sisters. I was so desperate to be loved by this boy that I would've done anything for him. I wore a semi-formal dress, a signature basic black cocktail style dress that all the girls wore for their first campus formal. I spent hours on my hair, makeup, and accessories. Everything had to be perfect.

William picked me up, and we went to a pre-party where they were doing keg stands and funneling beer. I had never been to a party like this, and both drinking methods had to be explained to me. Everyone at the party seemed really bothered by the fact that I was not drinking, including William. I just didn't see the point. The peer pressure was beginning to get to me, and I started to feel like I was different again, and not in a good way. I felt like a prude; like I didn't belong. Thankfully, it was time to leave for the real party, and I was just thrilled to be on the arm of a sophomore fraternity boy. The banquet hall was filled with large tables, and in the middle, there was a good-sized dance floor. I couldn't wait to dance with William. We sat down at a table, and then he left me to go make his rounds talking to new pledges, guests, and fraternity brothers. I didn't know a soul, and I was beginning to feel sad that I wasn't with my new girlfriends at my own Victory Party.

I sat there for a while, alone; and at one point, I happened to look up to see William out on the dance floor dancing with another girl. She was a tall, slender, beautiful blonde. I sat there watching them for about fifteen minutes until I finally realized he had no intention of returning to the table to be with me, and tears began to form in my eyes. A couple sitting at my table saw that I looked upset and asked me if I needed anything. With tears now streaming down my face, I said I needed a ride home. They said that they were leaving in a bit and would gladly take me to my dorm. I made it home in one piece except for my heart, which felt like it had split in half. I thought to myself, "Was this how college was going to be? Was I too much of a prude?" This was the point when I began to sink into my first depression.

I found myself skipping meals again and over-exercising to regain a sense of control in my life. I wasn't connecting with the girls in my sorority, so I decided to try out for the college dance team, "The Showgirls." I wanted to feel like I was a part of a group, and I wanted to dance again. I also threw myself into my studies once again. I made the Dean's List and the dance team in a matter of months. I was getting thinner and thinner, and I was beginning to experience terrible pain in my stomach. The pain was so severe after eating that I found myself on the floor of my dorm room several times a week, and it continued to get worse. Finally, I alerted my mother about how I was feeling, and she drove from Dallas to take me to the emergency room. The doctors found nothing wrong with me. No one realized at the time, including me, how negative emotions and emotional pain are stored in our gut and can affect us physically.

Life moved forward, as life does, and soon I met someone new. Greg, my next heartache in waiting. He was a fraternity boy my age and completely respected that I didn't drink and that I had made a choice to stay a virgin until marriage. This felt more like the relationships I had in high school — safe (but with extra butterflies). We spent every minute together. Greg made me laugh like no one I had ever met. We could spend hours in our dorm rooms making each other laugh. He was different from most boys I had met on campus because he wasn't focused on making me drink or trying to sleep with me. We would go to parties, and he would drink, but he was very comfortable with the fact that I didn't want to drink. I really felt like I was finally fitting in. Then around the middle of our freshman year, Greg told me that he had decided to transfer out of TCU to attend an out-of-state school. We only had about a month before he left at that point, and when he left for good, my heart hurt deeply. I internalized the entire situation, wondering to myself why everyone I loved always left me. Not having fully recovered from my previous depression, I fell into a deeper level of depression.

I went from having it all in high school — with a great group of friends who always made me feel safe and loved, a position as an award-winning lieutenant of the drill team, and a twin sister that supported me every step of the way — to being in college and not being able to keep a boyfriend or to connect with other girls. I felt so alone. I knew God existed because I went to church in high school and did everything right. Why did I feel so alone? Why did I feel so disconnected from God and from others? I completely fell apart, and my parents had to step in to get me help. They drove down, picked me up, and took me out of school to see a doctor about my depression. I coped by blocking most of it out because it was the first time I was showing the world that I wasn't perfect, and I didn't know how to handle it. With my mom and dad sitting on either side of me on the couch, the doctor analyzed my behavior. I did not like how the doctor made me feel or what he had to say. He said that in his opinion I could not handle going back to school.

He advised that I take a semester off which made me feel more isolated, depressed, and hopeless. This was only my freshman year of college. I had to finish, or I would look like a failure, and I could not deal with looking like a failure. So, despite the opinions of both the doctor and my parents about me going back to school, I returned to finish my freshman year.

It was 1993, and I was now in my sophomore year in college. What began as an opportunity to start fresh after a very difficult first year, turned into a year that would haunt me for years to come. As always, I tried to start the year off optimistic and adamantly holding on to what mattered to me the most at that time. My identity was almost like a badge I continually wore, and it was wrapped entirely around my virginity and my commitment to not drinking. I was so proud of these things that I should have just walked up to people and said, "Hi, my name is Vickie, and I am the non-drinking virgin on campus." Everyone already knew this because it was something I didn't hide. I now caution women about how important it is not to advertise these precious details because predators are always watching and listening.

Even though I was still terrified of dating and people who drank, I decided to attend a fraternity party with one of my sorority sisters. I must admit that I was hesitant because my first and only fraternity party during my freshman year sent me into my first downward spiral, but I was ready for a do-over, and I really wanted to fit in with my sorority sisters, so I went. The party was off campus, and I remember walking into a dark and smoky warehouse with large trashcans everywhere. My girlfriend explained that those trashcans housed trashcan punch, a very strong mix of alcohol and juice, and the alcohol was extremely hard to detect. I had heard stories of girls passing out after too much trashcan punch at frat parties, so I avoided it. A handsome guy with light hair and eyes came up to us and introduced himself as Robert. I had seen him on campus before. He was considered one of the popular guys. I don't remember what we talked about because I was out of my comfort zone and terrified. There I was again with everyone drinking, and I felt awkward, sweaty, and anxious. He must have picked up on my nervousness and suggested I try a drink he made. He said it tasted like cinnamon gum, that it didn't taste like alcohol and that it wasn't as strong as the trashcan punch. Caught between feeling out of place and wanting so much to finally fit in, I said "Ok." I took a sip, and he said, "No, you have to drink the entire thing." It was awful and burned my throat the entire way down. It was nothing like cinnamon gum. Everything got blurry after that. The next thing I remembered, I was lying in a very small bed, and the new song by Pearl Jam was playing somewhere in the distance — something about being held down and rising up — those words burned into my memory forever. Robert was on top of me, and I was trying to push him off, but he was taller, bigger, and stronger. I was so naive about sex that I didn't even know what was happening. His breath smelled like liquor, and by this point, that drink I had earlier had worn off completely. I realized that he was not going to stop. I remember staring at the ceiling and letting him do what he was doing. It was rough, painful, and I began to bleed. I'm not sure what came over me, why I just laid there, why I didn't fight him off. In retrospect, I realize I would repeat these patterns many times with men. I lost my non-drinking status, my virginity badge, and my power that night.

I woke up the next day in a filthy apartment with bugs running around on the floor and his roommates ready to get their morning drink on. The most difficult thing to understand was why I was not angry at first. I wasn't angry because I thought I was in love, and that more importantly, a man loved me. I equated sex with love. In my mind, we were dating, and this was a serious relationship. Then came the devastation. Robert didn't love me. He didn't even like me or want to get to know me as a person. I found out from one of his fraternity brothers later that I had been a bet. The price: $100. Robert had bet he could take me off the "V Team" or the "Virgin Team" as it was often called; a win that would boost his social status on campus and with his fraternity brothers. I was humiliated. The feeling of shame sunk deep into me. I could not let anyone know what had happened. I couldn't run the risk of this ruining my reputation any further, but somehow, I managed to destroy it anyway. I finished out my sophomore year in a drunken haze. I no longer had my perfect reputation, so I officially ditched every rule I had for myself. I had checked out. When I look back on the pictures from that year, I don't even recognize myself or the guys I was literally hanging all over in those pictures. My face went from fresh-faced and bright-eyed to sad and dull, with barely open eyes in every picture.

In the summer after my sophomore year, I went to my doctor for my yearly routine pap smear. I wasn't at all worried because this was such a quick and painless procedure. I waited the usual two weeks for my results, but instead of a card in the mail, I received a phone call from the doctor. I had an abnormal pap smear. My pap smears had always been normal before, but this time it was irregular. I was told I had something called the Human Papillomavirus (HPV) which she explained was a sexually transmitted disease producing different strains. I had the strain that could lead to cervical cancer.

What we didn't know or talk about back in the 1990s was that according to the Center for Disease Control and Prevention, nearly all cervical cancer is due to HPV. Now HPV is the most common sexually transmitted infection globally. Most sexually active people, who don't receive the HPV vaccination which was introduced in 2012, are infected at some point in their lives, and 80% of all women will get an HPV infection by the time they are 50 years old.

The doctor said I needed to have a biopsy, so I scheduled it for the following week. The procedure was quick with very little pain. While I was waiting for the results, I let my brain concoct these different diagnoses. When the biopsy results came back that these cells were CIN (Cervical Intraepithelial Neoplasia) Grade II precancerous cells on my cervix, my doctor explained that I was going to need a "LEEP" (Loop Electrosurgical Excision Procedure). She explained that the procedure would be done in the office with a laser and only a little discomfort. I was also told that this procedure should get rid of the abnormal cells and that I would just need to have a single follow-up appointment. One week later, I drove myself to the procedure feeling scared to death. The procedure itself wasn't that painful; what was more painful was the thought that I was no longer perfect.

I was no longer a virgin and now to add to the shame, I was damaged goods. I fixated on the fact that I had an STD that could potentially lead to cervical cancer. Was this punishment for losing my virginity, for breaking my pact with God? This is when I look back and wish that I had found one person in my life to talk to about all of this, rather than holding all of it in and harboring so much shame. I turned my back on God because I felt like I had disappointed him the most. This was when the biggest shift happened in my life.

At this point, I had the opportunity to take my situation and choose the path of forgiveness which meant forgiving myself for breaking my pact with God and forgiving the man who had decided that taking my virginity was worth money and popularity. Instead, I plunged deeper into self-loathing, shame and darkness. It was as if I had placed the invisible scarlet letter "V" on my chest and given myself a new identity — the identity of the perpetual victim.

My junior year and most of my senior year were a complete blur. Midway through my senior year, I met a man named Jonathon. He was ten years older, a fact I loved because I was ready to escape the college fraternity boy drama in hopes of finding my forever. My relationship with him gave me the excuse I needed to push all the pain from college down deeper inside. I thought this man was going to be my knight in shining armor who would save me from my past and heal my wounds. I graduated from TCU in the Spring of 1996 with my degree in Early Childhood Education.

# CHAPTER 3

# Perfectly Imperfect

"The thing that is really hard, and really amazing, is giving up on being perfect and beginning to work on becoming yourself."

- Anna Quindlen

It was the fall of 1996, and I had scored my dream job as a kindergarten school teacher and had my dream boyfriend, Jonathon. In my usual "take the most difficult and challenging road" fashion, I chose a school that was known as one of the lowest performing schools in the Dallas Independent School District. I was always convinced that I could make a difference and change the world. All I needed was the dream wedding and happily ever after to finish my fairytale plan. I was back to looking like I had it all on the outside, but once again on the inside, I was still feeling like an insecure college girl. It wasn't long until one thing began to bleed over to another, and my picture-perfect relationship was slowly becoming less perfect.

I was struggling with my body image and self-esteem, and Jonathon reinforced my insecurities, making me feel worse. He would push on my stomach and call me "Pillsbury dough girl." It took me years to ever show my stomach or let any man touch my belly as a result. I would soon develop a severe digestive issue, another example of my internal emotions manifesting in my physical body. As if poking me in the belly regularly wasn't enough, Jonathon was trying to convince me that I needed large fake breasts. My breasts were the only part of my body that I didn't hate. But after repeated comments about how much more attractive I would be with bigger breasts, I started to hate them too. I began to obsess about it. He told me that I would need them if we were ever going to get married. I was an elementary school teacher making 25 thousand dollars a year, and implants would cost me five months' salary. I felt like I could never be attractive enough for him to marry me, which was the goal I ultimately wanted to attain in order to stay on my timeline.

There were other things about Jonathon that contributed to my piling insecurities. He had more female friends than male friends, and they would be over at his house all the time. They would even stay over when I wasn't there. I would find random pieces of jewelry on the nightstand or under the bed and ask him whose they were. He would always tell me I was

overreacting and that these women were going through diffi-
cult times and needed a friend, so he would share his bed with
them but that they were fully clothed. I believed him, at least
I convinced myself I did. Deep down, I knew better, but I was
so afraid of losing him that I would let it go each time this sit-
uation came up. I was convinced that this was the best I could
ever do.

Because I was still starving myself and over-exercising,
one drink of alcohol always put me over the top. One night
when Jonathon and I were out at a bar, I only had one drink
but felt like I was going to get sick and pass out. Jonathon told
me that I needed to learn how to hold my liquor better and
took me to his truck, put me in the back seat and slammed the
door. I began to get sick. I laid there in my own vomit until
Jonathon was done partying with his friends in the bar. He was
so angry that I had gotten sick in his truck, that he made me get
it detailed the next day. Not once did he consider that I might
have choked on my own vomit in the back of his truck. Instead,
it took me months to make it up to him for leaving a mess in
his truck, and as he saw it, ruining his night. This was not love
in any form.

Later that same year, I received the news from my doctor
that I had additional pre-cancer cells (CIN grade II) and that I
would need a different in-office procedure called cryosurgery

which freezes the cells. I was told to just take it easy as this was another routine procedure. This was the hardest part for me since both work and working out were my outlets, and especially since I hadn't learned how to cope with my internal pain yet. The doctor reminded me how important it was to stay on top of my routine exams to stay healthy, but somewhere I had started to convince myself that I was probably not going to be able to have kids. It was my dream in life to have my own kids, especially to be in alignment with what I thought would be the perfect life. Convincing myself that my dream was not going to come true was a lie I kept telling myself; another lie that further prevented my healing.

Although I told Jonathon everything that I was dealing with physically, I didn't share any of the issues that were affecting me mentally. I continued to beat myself up on the outside, starving myself, over-exercising, and over-working to hide the pain I felt on the inside. I know that I was becoming less attractive to Jonathon because I was an emotional roller coaster. We were growing further apart, but I thought that getting engaged would fix all of that. I was convinced that he would be the only man who knew all my baggage and still marry me. I began putting the heavy pressure on him to propose. I even considered booking a wedding venue and church before he even popped the question. I had a timeline to stick to, but I began to slowly realize my timeline was self-imposed based on growing up in a city where everyone graduated from college, got married at 25, and had babies by 28.

In the winter of 1999, Jonathon proposed to me on a trip I had planned for him. I booked a cabin in the woods in Oklahoma for his birthday, a place that my family and I would go when I was a little girl and shared many happy memories. It was the perfect fairytale engagement. We arrived at our cabin late on a Saturday night. I had made a comment about how beautiful the lights were at the main lodge. We settled into our cabin, and I had just put my pajamas on when he said, "Why don't we go look at the lights at the lodge?" I was exhausted and wanted to just crawl into bed, but somehow, he convinced me to go with him. Once we got to the lodge, he said, "Let's go inside and look at the lights." I just wanted to hang in the car where it was warm, but he insisted, and I always did what he said. We went in and walked all the way to the back where I saw almost one hundred little candles lit along the dock in the back. We walked outside, and it started to sleet. Before I could say "let's go in," he dropped to one knee while music started to play. Once I heard our song by Shania Twain, I knew what was about to happen — Jonathon was finally proposing! And while standing in the sleet and cold, I said "YES!"

I went into crazy bridezilla wedding planning mode. Like everything I did in life, I was doing this 110%. I had the church, reception, photographer, florist, and dress all picked out within the first two months of my engagement. I was full speed ahead. Everything was lining up on my timeline just perfectly...well, sort of. The closer I got to the wedding date, the more nervous I became. I just assumed all brides got nervous, so I decided not to worry about it. I was in such a rush to meet this deadline I had created, I really didn't even consider that maybe I wasn't ready to get married. I was driven by the thought that I found someone who would marry me despite knowing all my baggage, and I had a specific timeline based on what I believed society was telling me. I ignored my intuitive feeling that something was off because I couldn't imagine calling off a wedding after all the planning and money spent; until the one night that changed everything — the last night we went out as a couple.

We were at a local bar in downtown Dallas celebrating with friends when something I said set Jonathon off. He decided that he was leaving with his friends and that I was going to have to find my own way home. Crying hysterically, I begged him not to leave me alone downtown. I had no way of getting home, and we certainly didn't have Uber back then. He left anyway, and I ended up having to call my parents to come get me. This was when I knew I had to call it quits. So, two months before I was supposed to get married, I called off the wedding. My parents were relieved. They knew it wasn't right either but weren't going to intervene. Jonathon was very upset, and despite what every girl said I was "supposed to do" with the ring, I gave it back. I didn't want to hold onto anything that would remind me of what I felt the world would only see as another failure.

As you will see in all my relationships to come, I never learned how to get rid of the mental baggage. The voices in my head kept telling me that I wasn't good enough, I wasn't perfect, I was flawed. My usual solution to controlling this inner critic was to hyper-focus on my physical appearance through over-dieting or over-exercising; but this time, I was obsessed with the idea that I had a fat belly and disproportionate breasts. I figured that if I got bigger fake breasts, then my stomach would appear flatter, and I would be more attractive to men. I used every penny I had in my small savings account for a boob job. I have few regrets in my life, and that's saying a lot with my history, but I honestly regret getting my breasts done. Not just because I figured out years later that my lack of confidence and love for myself was causing the distention in my gut, but because I, like so many women, suffer from complications of having two foreign objects in a healthy body. Ladies, if you are considering having your breasts done, make sure you are doing it for yourself and not someone else. And do your research.

# THE VALIDATION

# CHAPTER 4

# Numbing the Pain

"Numbing the pain for a while will make
it worse when you finally feel it."

- J.K. Rowling

W hen the 1990s were over, I hit the three-year burn out
with teaching, and I was ready for something new. I
went to the nail salon to have my nails done one afternoon and
began talking to my manicurist about how tired I was of teach-
ing school. A woman sitting next to me was eavesdropping
on the conversation and injected herself into it by asking me
questions. "What do you see yourself doing next? Do you think
you would like to be in a sales position?" she asked me. After
a few question-answer exchanges, the conversation felt more
like an informal interview. The woman was a district manager
for a pharmaceutical company, and after about an hour of chat-
ting in the nail salon, she invited me to a formal interview for
a position with her company. As it turns out, pharmaceutical

companies love hiring teachers because they are willing to work for little pay, have teaching skills, and typically have a lot of energy. It took almost a month to complete the rounds of interviews with various people within the company before I was offered a job as a pharmaceutical rep. I was very excited about the change and was looking forward to meeting new people and the chance to grow in a new opportunity.

I was making more money and had a company car at my disposal, so I decided to move out of my parents' back house and into my own place. Ironically, one of the primary drugs to represent to doctors was an anti-depressant, which I delivered with a positive attitude and a big smile. To everyone else, everything looked like it was going well and that my life was running smoothly. However, despite appearances, I was slipping into a deeper state of depression on the inside. Independent and on my own again, I started going out every weekend. It didn't take long before my old patterns emerged, and I began making bad choices with both alcohol and men. I would get a rush from trying to get as many men I could to talk to me and hit on me, with the goal of going home with one at the end of the night. I was using my body to allure men, and it worked. It made me feel powerful and alive, but the feeling of power was only temporary. It was the equivalent of taking a drug. When a guy gave me attention, I would feel on top of the world and then by the following day, I would hit rock bottom from shame and self-disgust, sometimes laying in the fetal position for hours crying until I couldn't cry anymore. In my mind, I would replay the disgusting things I allowed these men to do to me, then convince myself that it was my choice and that I enjoyed it. After hours of self-loathing, I would drag myself out of bed, go to the gym and beat my body up with some crazy intense workout. The pain was always there, no matter what I did to escape it.

A personal trainer friend of mine asked me if I was all right because I seemed so angry during my workouts. As opaque as I thought I was to those around me, I couldn't hide my pain. I desperately needed validation from men, yet I was literally starving for love. In my mind, if I had sex with these men, they would want to be with me, but as much as I always hoped that these men would call me the next day, they never did. They didn't want anything to do with me. In retrospect, I understand that I was repeating my first sexual experience over and over again. I was perpetuating my own cycle of abuse to avoid the real pain buried deep within me, and I abused myself as a twisted form of retribution.

One night stood out from the rest. This time the pain and self-loathing set in right away, as opposed to the typical 24-hour window before the breakdown began. The guy I met that night was a fitness trainer. He was big, muscular and extremely strong. After spending some time together, he asked me to come back to his place. He made drinks, and we listened to music and talked. I felt like we were making a real connection and when we started kissing, it was sweet, romantic and tender. Kissing led to making out and then out of nowhere, his energy suddenly shifted. He became forceful and had me pinned face down with his huge frame. Scared, I tried to push him off, but I couldn't get him to stop. No matter how many times I said no, he ignored me and continued. I felt like I was back in college with no control and no way to protect myself. Less than two minutes went by, though it felt like a lifetime had passed. He abruptly finished, told me to get out of his bed, and out of his house. My mind spinning, I stumbled around trying to find my clothes and heard him say, "You are a whore."

Thankfully I had driven my car to his place, so I wasn't stranded. As I shared earlier, the oh so convenient Uber didn't exist back then, and I would have been in an even worse situation otherwise. Once again, I found myself doing the awful "walk of shame" to my apartment from my car wearing the same clothes I had on the night before. Sadly, at this point in my life, they were becoming second nature. When I got to my car, the floodgates opened. The thought of reporting this guy never crossed my mind because somewhere deep down, I believed

I deserved this. I needed help and badly. I needed guidance and insight from someone who understood and could help me understand why I kept giving my power away to these men and kept hurting myself in this way. However much I needed that help, I didn't seek it out. It seemed much easier to stay in this vicious cycle, even though my body was beginning to suffer physically as a result of my mental and psychological state.

Life moved on and soon it was time again for another bi-yearly medical exam. The results came in, and I got the dreaded call. The abnormal cells previously identified had spread over a larger portion of my cervix and were now CIN early stage III, and I would need a more invasive surgery – Cold Knife Conization – to address it. I was thrown into a spin cycle of guilt and self-flagellation asking myself a million unanswerable questions, "Why is this happening again? Was my behavior with men causing this?"

Thankfully, I was referred to one of the best oncologists in Dallas, and as a pharmaceutical rep, I had great insurance. I would have to go under anesthesia this time, so they could remove a larger piece of my cervix and then I would have to be on bed rest for a week. This news sent me into a state of panic and anxiety. I had so much work to do and couldn't possibly skip a week of working out. Even though it occurred to me that God was telling me to slow down and heal, I didn't listen.

Looking back, I wish I had used that time to let go of the pain, anger, and resentment that I had towards men. It would have done a great deal of good and might have changed the direction I was headed in life. I woke up from the anesthesia to my doctor and parents standing over me. From our conversations during my pre-surgery appointments, the doctor intuitively had picked up on my pattern of over-doing. As I laid there, I heard the doctor repeating his orders for recovery to my parents to ensure that I stayed on bedrest and out of the gym until I healed. Jokingly, he said that he never wanted to see me in his office again and then turning more serious said he felt that he was successful in getting all the lesions and wanted me to stay healthy so that I could have the children I dreamed of having. Listening and outwardly optimistic for their benefit, inside I still believed that it wasn't going to happen, and I wouldn't ever be able to have kids. Though he assured me I would be fine, I had created this story in my head to cope with the chance that I might have to go through these procedures over and over again. I had begun to wholeheartedly believe my own version of my fabrication because I thought it would make it easier rather than end up being disappointed. I thought I was protecting myself, but instead, I was literally perpetuating the cycle of disease (dis-ease) inside of me.

I was not an easy patient, and especially unhappy being sedentary for an entire week. The hardest part of my healing process was that my predicament forced me to take the time to reflect and assess my life, and I had to ask myself some hard questions. "Was my behavior with men and the abuse I was inflicting on my body causing these recurrences? Did I deserve all of this as a punishment from God?" I couldn't seem to get a straight answer from myself or from the universe, and I didn't have anyone to talk through what was going on, to shed light on a possible answer. As a result, I started to feel like I was completely alone, again. The only thing I could hear ringing through my head was the damaged goods story I had been telling myself for years.

# CHAPTER 5

# Prey Not Pray

"You have been criticizing yourself for
years, and it hasn't worked. Try approving
of yourself and see what happens."

- Louise Hay

Looking back, I genuinely believe that there are two differ-ent energy vibrations a woman can emit; one is an energy that attracts good men who have a genuine interest in getting to know her as a person, and the other is an energy that attracts lesser or predatory men that will take advantage of her. More on that later.

At this point in my life, while I was wrapping up my 20's and heading into my 30's, I had completely turned my back on my faith. The girl who lived for church and the friendships she found there, now found it easier and normal not to believe in anything. The girl who didn't need alcohol and was saving herself for marriage now found comfort in booze and having casual sex with men. I had grown comfortable with categorizing myself as "easy," "fast," or "a slut" because I was not honoring my body or respecting myself as a woman. It was so much easier to find darkness. The light seemed too far away.

I felt like I needed yet another fresh start with a new job. It was another pattern I had developed that enabled me to continue to sidestep my own reality. Changing jobs allowed me to mentally disconnect from the pain, anger, and fear and contributed to my feeling of control over the things I felt I could not control. I decided to become a certified personal trainer. What better way to feed my addiction every day? Now I had an excuse and a real reason to beat my body up, and no one would know that I was struggling with my body image. Of course, my issues with food resurfaced as well. I was completely consumed with perfecting my outer appearance to hide my perceived imperfections and inadequacies. I was eating an average of a thousand calories a day and exercising two hours a day, every day. I received constant compliments from everyone because I was the personification of what a personal trainer is expected to look like. I had restricted my calorie intake and pushed myself so hard that I was close to passing out at any given time while training clients. I was down to 100 pounds at 5 feet 5 inches, which was nowhere close to being healthy or sustainable. I had completely fallen out of love with myself and focused wholly on the wrong things.

One Saturday night, typical by most standards, I was feeling particularly down and insecure. Tired of feeling that way, I opted for my go-to routine to cheer myself up; go out dancing, lose myself in the music and block my reality out of my mind. The memory of exactly what I was wearing that night will forever be burned in my brain. I wore a pair of dressy, fitted, black satin shorts and a fitted gold tank top with black high heeled stilettos, the style of shoes I had learned men preferred. Still, I looked rather conservative compared to most other girls out that Saturday night in Dallas. The club scene was hopping, and the wait and line to get in were long. Lucky for us, in typical nightclub fashion, based on our looks alone, the bouncer chose my girlfriends and me to cut the line and go right inside. Excited and happy to be inside, we made a beeline for the dance floor. It was dark, and the smell and smoke of a fog machine filled the room. The strobe lights illuminated the room with a rhythmic pulse, and I started to recognize many of the faces as belonging to people I knew, many of them being men grinding up against women I knew were not their wives. Sadly, this was normal in my world, and it barely registered in my mind as out of place anymore.

The four of us made a pact to look out for each other like we always did at the club, and then we scoped out where we wanted to camp out on the dance floor. Our favorite area to dance was one of the raised platforms that had a pole, and we got lucky, finding one that wasn't yet occupied. Jumping up on the platform, we started dancing like nobody was watching. I didn't have a buzz, but that never stopped me from dancing. I never needed alcohol to dance, even in front of complete strangers. A guy I knew from the gym, who was married, came up to the platform, handed me a drink and said, "Hey, I bought you a drink." I didn't think anything of it since I knew him fairly well, so I didn't hesitate to accept it and drink it. That was the last thing I remember.

My head felt heavy; I couldn't lift it off my pillow, and the light hurt my eyes. I knew immediately this wasn't a typical hangover and that something was off. I had only had one drink that I could remember. I had no memory of how I got home, but at least I was at home. I finally pulled my head up off the pillow just high enough to see the floor beneath me. There were huge muddy footprints on the carpet next to my bed. I had clothes on, but no underwear. I knew something had happened — my body didn't feel right.

Suddenly there was loud banging at my door, which sounded like thunder that shook the entire room because my head was throbbing so badly. I made my way to the door to unlock it and found it was one of my friends who I had been dancing with the night before. Alison was the one who always made sure we stayed together and always had my back. She was upset and asked me why I had left and wasn't answering my cell phone. Just then, it occurred to me that I didn't know where my phone or purse was. Luckily, Alison located my purse and my wallet. Knowing at that moment I didn't have to stop payment on credit cards or go get a new driver's license was somehow comforting, even though I was still unsure as to what had actually happened to me. Thankfully, I also realized I had possession of my keys, but we couldn't find my phone.

Miraculously, just then, my mother called Alison's phone and told her she was worried because someone had found my cell phone discarded, laying cracked in the street outside of an apartment complex, and called the first number in my call history. Ironically, that would be my mother's number.

At that point in my life, I was so disconnected from my family. I didn't think they would understand what I was going through, so I kept them at a distance. They had the life I expected to have: get married in your 20's, have kids, and live happily ever after. Instead, I had gone down a different path and spent my time partying at nightclubs into all hours of the night. I was definitely not the definition of the golden child.

I assured my mom that I was fine and had just dropped my phone and for her not to be worried. I didn't want her to know that I didn't remember how I got home, or how my phone got to that apartment complex located on the other side of Dallas from the dance club. Alison tried to convince me to go see a doctor to make sure I was okay and not physically injured. However, I was in such a deep pit of shame that I convinced myself that whatever had happened was my fault, and I refused to get out of bed. I felt I couldn't take legal action even if I should. I felt I didn't have a safe place to fall or anyone I could call. In my head, I could almost hear those that loved me saying, "What did you do this time Vickie?" I was my own worst enemy at this point, deciding on reactions and outcomes before they could happen. This was the first time in my life that I truly wanted to die. I laid in bed trying to put the pieces together, still unsure of what really had happened and asking myself over and over, "Did I ask for this?"

Day two came, and I decided to stay in bed another day, canceling both classes and clients. I was in a full-on depression and struggling to climb out. When I finally pulled myself together and resurfaced, I headed back to the gym per my usual coping routine; but this time, I couldn't even muster the strength to take it out on myself via a workout like I had always done in the past. This time was different, and I was struggling badly. It took more energy to be positive with my clients and all my efforts to maintain the perfect facade were ineffective. The glass was cracking, and there was no hiding it.

One of the trainers, Brian, noticed something was amiss and offered to talk if I thought it would help. Relieved and exhausted with carrying the weight alone, I decided to bare my soul and told him everything that I could remember about that fateful Saturday night. For the first time in my life, I felt I could trust a man, and as a result, Brian would become a source of light and stability for me in the coming years and quite possibly one of my guardian angels.

## CHAPTER 6

# 50 Shades of Terrible

"You are the best mistake that stopped
happening to me. Thank you for the lessons."

- Najwa Zebian

Fast forward to 2004, and at 30 years old, one would think I would have learned from my previous wake up calls that I needed to take a strong look at what I was doing to continue to attract the same type of man. I do believe that something greater than me — God, the universe, something — was trying to get my attention and show me that I was worthy of love and deserved better. Instead, I continued to ignore these cosmic interventions of hope and help. Probably not surprisingly, Carter rolled onto the scene.

From "Vickie, I love you so much that I would die for you," to "Vickie, shut the f*ck up," and "You are such a little whore Vickie," was the roller coaster ride I found myself on. The highs were so high, sweet, and intoxicating, but the lows were so low, hateful, and toxic. Most of the men I spent time with in my life were alcoholics — some with an added narcissistic personality disorder — and Carter was a classic alcoholic. One thing that they all had in common was their ability, in the beginning, to make me feel like I was the best thing that ever happened to them. So naturally, my whole-hearted self always saw the best in these men, falling hook, line, and sinker.

We began dating in the period of my life that centered around constantly going out, and I was using alcohol to numb my emotional pain. Thankfully my drinking was situational, whereas Carter's drinking was an addiction. He used every excuse in the book to drink; a favorite was that he had to go out because it was a buddy's birthday party, and he couldn't let him down. It was something every night of the week. I got used to him lying about who he was with or where he was going, and he often never came home at the end of the evening. Rumors circulated, and I knew that there were other women. He would receive phone calls from girls and say the calls were work-related. Though I knew better, I wanted to see the best in him and forced myself to believe him.

When we went out together, I would only have one drink max because there would always be a fight at the end of the night when I suggested that it was time to go home. Carter always had a way of being the life of the party, while making me look like I was the bad guy or the "buzz kill." He would invite the entire bar back to his house without even considering my feelings and apologize to his new "friends" for my boring behavior. The male ego and alcohol are a bad combo when it comes to drinking and driving.

No matter how hard I begged him to let me drive, Carter would somehow always win the argument. Then came the drive home from hell which consisted of him speeding over 100 miles an hour, screaming at me about how worthless I was, and me begging him to slow down through the tears streaming down my face. Thank God, I made it home alive.

Once we got home, if people were over at the house, I would go straight to the bedroom. I was sick of the adolescent behaviors that manifested themselves in loud music and excessive alcohol use late into the night. If it happened to be a night when people were not coming over to continue the party, the situation would often be worse because he would beat his dogs and punish me by making me sleep on the couch. Usually, a night like that was followed up by a day of me walking on eggshells around Carter to keep the peace. He never became physically abusive to me, but his behavior made me feel like it was only a matter of time. Thankfully, I left before things progressed to physical abuse. Many people aren't so lucky.

My anger and shame surrounding my past with men was growing silently on the inside and manifested a masculine side of me that began to take over. I wore jeans and t-shirts and refused to wear skirts, dresses, or pink. I started lifting heavy in my workouts and put on weight in an attempt to protect myself. However, it was all a smokescreen. Although I portrayed this tough, strong woman on the outside, I was still the same vulnerable, sensitive girl with a huge heart that feared getting hurt again by a man. I was so desperate to feel loved that I even tried having a relationship with a woman. Something about it felt safe, but not for long. I quickly realized that this was another attempt to avoid the real work I needed to do to heal my relationship with men. I still hadn't done any work on myself. It seemed easier to focus on maintaining a relationship that was dysfunctional than to be alone and do the work to attract the right kind of man into my life. Being with anyone versus being alone to avoid feeling the pain seemed the easier choice.

Most of the men in my past had issues with alcohol, so when I met Mark, who didn't drink at all, things seemed different. Unfortunately, he had other destructive and narcissistic behaviors, such as an extreme need for control, and a difficult time staying monogamous. In retrospect, I think I would have preferred an alcohol problem to his twisted "50 Shades of Terrible" sexual addiction. At first, Mark seemed steady and even-keeled, but that facade began to fade rather quickly, and things began to change after about a month of dating.

We both enjoyed working out, and we would go to the gym together regularly. One Saturday, I told him that I wanted to show him an exercise I learned for working the core, and it required a heavier medicine ball and a stability ball. He agreed to try, and while he positioned himself on the stability ball, I grabbed a 15-pound medicine ball, a completely solid ball with no give. Once he was ready, I started the exercise by gently tossing the ball to him, which he gently tossed back. At this point, I made a mistake, telling him he was throwing like a girl. When he leaned back to throw the ball back again, I knew I was in trouble by the look on his face. It was pure rage. The ball hit me in the nose, and I instantly felt dizzy and nauseous. Like a reenactment of the famous Marsha Brady scene from the Brady Bunch show, I yelled: "You broke my nose!" He replied, "No I didn't, quit your crying." The gush of blood followed immediately, confirming my fears. Mark had broken my nose. It was my first sign that this man had an anger problem, but once again, I didn't heed the warnings.

We arrived at the emergency room, and the nurses at check-in were instantly suspicious of my story of how it happened. I am fairly certain they thought he had hit me rather than it being the result of a gym accident. The doctor on call rammed a rod up each side of my nose, packed it and sent me on my way. To this day I can't breathe clearly, and I live with a deviated septum. Yet another reminder of past lessons.

The medical bills started to come in, and Mark refused to help pay, even though he was well off and regularly spent thousands of dollars on his gun collection. He had two oversized safes that were floor to ceiling in height where he stored them. He was not a hunter and didn't even frequent the gun range; he just collected — a manifestation of his ego. Like clockwork, every week he would take them out, clean them, point them at me and laugh, with the retort, "They aren't loaded, babe."

There were so many signs I should have paid attention to. He was cruel and mean-natured, once spraying Windex in a puppy's face as punishment for peeing on the kitchen floor when we were dog-sitting for a relative. To this day, I feel sick to my stomach when I hear the title "50 Shades of Grey." Marketing around that story highlighted it as a fun, fantasy-filled life, something to try with their significant other to spice up a couple's sex life. Unfortunately, in my experience, being with a man who truly gets satisfaction from dominating a woman, there is nothing romantic, fun, or healthy about that sort of relationship. Men like these are nothing like Christian Grey, the lead male character, who is portrayed as alluring and sexy. The book was written by a woman, so he is portrayed as a man who grows to care for Ana, the female lead character, rather than just seeing her as someone to dominate. I assure you that men like Mark, who are into this, are entirely in it for themselves and are looking for the feeling of dominance, power, and control. It is about them getting what they want with no regard for their partner, and there is nothing sexy or romantic about that.

Mark was the first one to introduce me to pornography, and he required me to watch it with him. That's when the lines between making love, having sex, and being assaulted began to become blurry. I felt pressured to look and perform like these women in the videos. He would order outfits that consisted of chains, dog collar chokers, thigh chokers, and then tell me to put them on. He told me exactly what he wanted to do and if I was uncomfortable, he didn't care. He disconnected emotionally, and it felt like he went to an alternate universe and treated me as if I was one of his business deals, an asset and something he owned. He would take immense pleasure from leaving bruises or handprints on me. After having sex, he would spank me as hard as possible with an open hand to see how much of an outline he could make on my skin, laughing as he left his mark and obviously pleased with himself. Somehow, I had convinced myself this was normal and that this was love since I had never experienced anything different. I did anything and everything to make sure a man was happy and satisfied because that is what I felt I was supposed to do. I had never experienced a man holding me or cuddling with me the way my girlfriends talked about it.

Things were getting worse, and he was always looking to take things up a notch. One night, I woke up from a dead sleep and Mark was forcing himself on me. Half asleep, out of the corner of my eye, I thought I saw what looked like a tripod set up next to the bed. It was a video stand, and I hadn't ever seen it before. I recall saying something about it at the time, and he told me I was seeing things. The next day I brought it up again, but he told me I was crazy. He was so emphatic, and I started to believe him. For some reason, it was always easier to believe the stories men told me about me, rather than to listen to my own intuition or what I knew to be true.

I stayed in this relationship for almost a year, a lot longer than was typical for me. Mark would always ask me to go on trips with him on the weekends, which of course seemed like a nice break, but it wasn't really a request. I knew I was expected to go every time. One trip he arranged for us was for six days, which was longer than usual. This trip was to be the event that ended our relationship. Due to the length of time I would have to be gone, I told him that I could not go because I would be unable to take that much time away from my clients. He was pissed and called me a spoiled brat. "Any woman would drop everything to go on a trip like this with me!" he said.

He made me feel so guilty for saying I couldn't go, and he didn't care or understand that I would have to give up income to make the trip work. I told him that if he paid for those clients I would miss, then I would be able to go. He just laughed and informed me that he was going without me. In all honesty, I should not have been surprised considering his refusal to assist with the medical bills after he broke my nose.

So I stayed to work, and he went on the trip without me. Near the end of the trip, I received a call from him. I was at the end of one of my training sessions, so I was able to pick up, but what I heard on the other end was not the usual "Hey babe!" but instead, I heard him talking about the hot babe he had hooked up with on the trip. He had not intended to call me. This was an accidental call, a "butt dial." He was on the airplane on the runway ready to take off to come back to Dallas and was recapping his trip with a male passenger sitting next to him. He was going on and on about how amazing this woman was with "big tits" whom he spent the weekend with. I couldn't listen any longer. I hung up. I felt sick…a feeling I knew far too well at this point.

When he got home that evening, I confronted him. He called me "crazy" and a "liar," and he tried to make me second guess what I knew I had heard. The typical controlling behaviors of narcissists are often employed to keep their object feeling weak and needy. I knew he was the one who was lying; and for the first time, I knew I deserved better, so I ended it. Months later, he resurfaced with a text telling me he was watching a video of me and that it was "so hot"— the video from the night I thought I had seen a tripod. It was more confirmation that I had been in the hands of yet another predator. The thought of that video in his hands haunts me to this day.

# CHAPTER 7

# Sweaty Money

"Whatever you fear most has no power.
It is your fear that has the power."

- Oprah Winfrey

I not only allowed men to take advantage of me in my personal life, but I also let my low self-esteem and lack of confidence/self-worth bleed over into my business as well. From 2004 through 2006, my clientele was predominantly men; married white men with money, power, and connections. Obviously, not all the men I trained crossed the line of impropriety, but those that did cross it, did so with no fear of repercussion; in part, because they were used to getting their way and in part because I was not strong enough to put them in their place. I had not established strong boundaries, something I struggled with my entire life. I was coming from a place of fear and had convinced myself that if I told them to stop, they would stop training with me and it would incapacitate me financially.

One client liked to exercise his power in a very degrading way. He was a married, successful CEO who had the means to pay me for his training sessions in advance, but instead, insisted on paying me cash at the end of each session. He would keep the money tucked into the waistband of his shorts and hand it to me, dripping wet from his sweat. Unfortunately, his controlling and inappropriate behavior didn't stop there. He would sit in his car conducting business calls during our session time leaving me waiting, and then when he finally decided he was ready to work out, would enter the gym and snap his fingers at me to begin. He would then tell me what *he* wanted to work out that day and where *he* wanted me to stand. One of his favorite demands was to have me stand between his legs when he was doing core exercises, and not a session went by when he didn't ask me what I was wearing under my leggings. I became a pro at redirecting, deflecting, laughing off and attempting to avoid all sexually explicit requests or comments, but I still wasn't able to set the boundaries I needed to truly curb his behavior. However, as bad as this man's behavior was towards me, he wasn't nearly the worst offender.

I had another extremely wealthy client, but this one insisted on taking me to lunch instead of working out. I initially wasn't too concerned and in fact, thought it was fairly harmless because he was 40 years older than me, old enough to be my grandfather. I did what I could to impress upon him the benefits of a healthy lifestyle, explaining how important it was that he regularly exercised since he was an older man with on-going health issues. Sadly, instead of listening to my advice, he used his position and the leverage of money to convince me that I needed to heed his requests, constantly reminding me that he pre-paid for his sessions a month in advance. At this point, it actually occurred to me that the CEO client with his sweaty cash was a safer situation because at least I could cancel his session and not be held accountable by a pre-paid session.

I felt extremely uncomfortable with this client taking me to lunch not only because as a trainer, it wasn't what I should be doing, but because he was also married. I was fairly certain his wife would not appreciate her husband regularly dining with his 30-something-year-old fitness trainer. There were days I was able to convince him to stay in the gym and work out, using the argument that I had spent a lot of time on his work-out program. It should have been no surprise, but he attempted to take further advantage of me during those sessions, by trying to touch me inappropriately when I demonstrated an exercise for him. I spent the entire session ducking and dodging his advances. As things progressed, his use of psychological manipulation increased as well. When he thought I had put on weight, he quickly brought it to my attention. I started to dress in baggy clothes, with every inch of my body covered. He then complained that I had too much clothing on and reminded me that he was paying me to look a certain way. I felt powerless. I was convinced that if I drew boundaries and confronted him on his inappropriate behavior, he would stop training with me, and I would be unable to pay my bills. The stress of dealing with this abuse from my clients was taking its toll; it got so bad that I came down with a terrible case of shingles. My body always found a way to let me know that it had enough.

Things finally came to a head one Friday. He had convinced me that it was going to be a "lunch workout" that day and that he would drive us to the restaurant. This was a new request because usually, I would follow him in my own car. After lunch, we returned to the parking lot at the gym, and as I was about to get out of the car, he grabbed my bare leg and slid his hand to the upper part of my thigh. I was very nervous and didn't know what to do at that moment. His hand was now stroking my leg, and he said he would pay off all my debt if I spent one night in bed with him. "I am not sure if I can still get it up, but I want to touch your body all night long," He said. I froze, terrified. I couldn't speak or move. Then he said, "Think about it."

I couldn't get out of the car fast enough, immediately running inside the gym to find the owner. I told him what had happened, expecting at least some sort of protective or horrified response. Instead, he told me I was a fool to turn the deal down and that I should have "taken one for the team" and that it was only one night. Stunned and hurt, I didn't realize at the time that his words would be an eerie foreshadowing of one of the worst nights of my life.

Me at my tap recital at age 8 in 1982

Me at age 12 in 1986

Me as a high school drill team lieutenant at age 16 in 1990

"The Griffith Twins" at age 17 - high school drill team in 1992

My high school graduation at age 18 in the spring of 1992

Me as a TCU Showgirl at age 19 in 1993

TCU graduation in the spring of 1996

My 30th Birthday in 2004

Me and Pepe in 2008

Me leading the One Billion Rising global movement in 2014

My first victory in 2017

My victory dance in 2018

# THE VOICE

# CHAPTER 8

# Ascending the Mountain

"Today is my favorite day."

- Brian

It was December of 2006 and Brian, the one man in my life I trusted fully, my friend and confidant I bared my soul to, and the one man whose name isn't changed in this book, left Dallas to follow his dream to climb Mount Hood in Portland Oregon. Brian was a trainer at the gym where we worked and was the kind of person who always went above and beyond. He was the guy with an incredible soul. He fed the homeless in the alley behind the gym and gave the squirrels expensive organic store-bought nuts. He was the man who reminded me daily to never stop dancing and was my soon to be guardian angel.

My favorite "Brian Story" was an adventure to the hospital after one of my clumsy mishaps in the gym. There was a metal, spiral staircase in the middle of the gym floor leading up to the trainer office and it had sharp metal edges under the steps. I would bump into them on occasion if I wasn't purpose-fully careful while gathering equipment for a client. The guys I worked with would joke that they needed to put bumpers on the stairs to "Vickie proof" the gym. One day I was stretching a client out underneath the staircase because the training floor was full. I was preoccupied with my task and completely forgot the staircase was above me until I stood up abruptly and hit one of the sharp edges. I didn't realize that anything had hap-pened until the blood started pouring down my face. Brian, who was standing a few feet away, told me to sit down, and he went to grab a towel. He dismissed both our clients and rushed me to the Emergency Care down the street. When we arrived, we sat and waited with all the patients, many who were cough-ing and sneezing. Clearly, everyone was suffering from a bad cold or the flu, and it wasn't the best place to be. Brian looked at me and said, "We are out of here." He called one of his cli-ents, a doctor, who generously offered to see me at his hospital office on the other side of town if we could get there within 30 minutes. Brian drove as fast as he could to get us there in time. Paying no attention to the speed limit, we were suddenly pursued by loud sirens and flashing lights…we were getting pulled over by a police officer. Brian quickly told the officer that I had a terrible head wound, and we needed an escort to the hospital. With sirens blazing, that's exactly what we got.

The doctor stitched me up while Brian waited and gave me specific instructions not to wash my hair for a few days. Then the doctor placed a giant blue shower cap on my head to keep the wound sanitary. Obviously, I looked ridiculous, and Brian couldn't resist ribbing me for it. He always knew how to cheer me up and make me feel like everything would be ok. Sadly, that was one of the last times I spent time with Brian.

Brian was a personal trainer with a passion for mountain climbing. He had climbed several dangerous peaks, so climbing Mount Hood was not considered a difficult climb. The first part of the climb went well. The Saturday night before his group was due to descend, I had a terrible dream that there had been an accident. I woke up the next morning to a terrible reality. Brian and his two fellow climbers hadn't made it to base camp, and they were missing. A massive search was executed, but only one of the climber's bodies was found in a man-made snow cave. Brian and the other climber were never found. Our close-knit gym family was devastated by the loss of our friend, our brother. Though the search teams continued to look for the two missing climbers, there was very little hope that they would be found. We were forced to begin the grieving process and say our goodbyes. At some point early in the process, someone gave me the number of a woman who was available to help us in the grieving process. I had no way of knowing at the time how much this woman would impact my life. To this day, every time I enter a situation that could be potentially dangerous whether it be dating, friendship, or work-related, fire trucks with loud alarms appear. I am convinced that my guardian angel Brian is sending these warning signals to protect me.

# CHAPTER 9

# I Found My Guru

"She had not known the weight
until she felt the freedom."

- Nathaniel Hawthorne, *The Scarlet Letter*

It was now 2007. I had just lost a very dear friend and was deep into my grieving process. At some point, I realized it was time to get some help letting go of the past so that I could move forward. I picked up the phone and called the number I had been given and made an appointment. I didn't know if the woman was considered a therapist or a counselor because all I had was her name and number on a piece of paper. When I spoke to her on the phone, she asked me to come prepared with the information of the exact day and time of my birth. Of course, I knew my birthday, but I had no clue what time I was born, but my mother did. And boy, was I glad I called her; she shared a story about my birth that I had never heard before. My mother's water broke early in the morning on May 21, 1974, over a month early. My twin sister, Mandy, arrived into the world at 7:13 pm and was placed in a warming box, and both my parents and doctor thought they were done. Then the doctor told the anesthesiologist, "Hold on…we have another baby in here." My parents thought he was joking because he had that type of humor. Apparently, I was in a small ball, up high, hiding from the world; they never heard another heartbeat during my mother's entire pregnancy! At 7:30pm, I arrived into the world. Perhaps my birth story began to explain why I had always felt different, but I still had no clue why this counselor/therapist needed this information…I would soon find out.

I arrived on time for my first appointment, which was very rare for me (And since now I knew I was late to my own birth, this was even more intriguing to me). I would come to notice over time that even though she lived 30 minutes away, I would always arrive right on time for our weekly appointments. I walked in the door for my first visit and felt an instant feeling of warmth; not like the heat from an external source like a heater but more of an inner warmth that felt energizing and soothing. I sat down on her couch directly across from her. The first thing she said to me was, "So tell me, why are you pushing away men?" Stunned, I was taken completely off guard. How could she possibly know? Could she see that invisible scarlet letter "V" for victim I was still wearing on my chest? She repeated the question. I responded this time and told her it was very difficult for me to talk about and asked her how she could tell that I was pushing away men. She said that she was picking up some energy in my second chakra. My head was spinning. "My second whatra??" I obviously had so much to learn. She explained that my "Birth Chart" and the energy she was picking up on revealed that I was holding onto a lot of anger as it pertained to my health and men. At that moment I knew this woman, whom I would soon refer to as my "Spiritual Director," had a gift.

Intrigued and excited, I set a weekly appointment with her despite my on-going financial struggle. Yet somehow, I always managed to have just enough extra to go see her. We worked on a new technique each week that allowed me to release the years of anger, shame, fear, and guilt that I was carrying around and hiding all the way down into the tissues of my cells. She was the first person who taught me how to really meditate, or "go-to level" as she called it. I began meditating every day, mid-day between clients.

One day, I showed up for my appointment, and her first question was, "Have you seen your doctor lately for a cervical check-up?" I admitted I was past due for a check-up. She told me it was imperative to call and make an appointment right then, while I was sitting there. She was obviously picking up on something, so I took her seriously, made the appointment, and I was glad I did. The routine checkup and pap smear results showed I had a large mass of suspicious cells on my cervix, and the doctor wanted to do a follow-up biopsy. Initially, my heart sank, but this time I realized I had some new techniques to help me cope. I meditated regularly and took high amounts of turmeric to lower the inflammation. I heeded her advice and also did a Reiki energy healing session a few days before the biopsy.

The Reiki session was nothing I had ever experienced before. The Reiki Master who performed the session explained to me that I would lie face up on a table while he realigned my energy systems throughout my body without touching me. I tried to remain open and optimistic as it began, and I instantly felt the warmth. It was very similar to the warmth I felt during my sessions with my Spiritual Director. Halfway into the session, I suddenly felt a strong pulling sensation out of the right side of my temple and then a sensation that felt like an object about the size of a gumball shoot out of my body and hit the wall directly in front of me. When the session was over, the practitioner told me the areas where he felt an energetic change: my right temple and second chakra, where my female sex organs were located. I was floored. You can't make this stuff up. Incredibly, ten days after my procedure, I received the news from my doctor that my biopsy came back clear. I didn't know if it was the sessions with my Spiritual Director, the session with the Reiki Master, or the supplements I was taking, but what I was sure of was that I was ready to keep practicing these techniques to stay healthy.

My Spiritual Director felt it was also important for me to get back in touch with my feminine side. I had no idea what she meant initially. I hated dresses and despised pink. She had mentioned that on my first appointment with her, I was really giving off a masculine energy full of anger and frustration. She brought up many times how I was unintentionally pushing away men. She wanted me to let go of the anger I had towards the men who hurt me, thoroughly heal, and learn how to accept love and give love again.

Her next suggestion caused my jaw to hit the floor. Belly dancing. Belly dancing, really? It sounded so silly and girly and like a terrible and very uncomfortable idea for me to swallow. She told me I needed to get back in touch with the music, hip movements, and freedom of movement. I did still love to dance, but it had been so long since I had. However, I was learning that if something made me feel uncomfortable, then I should probably do it.

Less than a week later, on a Monday, I had noticed a flyer on our gym bulletin board that I had never seen before. It was a new class the gym was offering called, "The Art of Exotic

Dancing for Everyday Women." I read the description, and although it wasn't exactly belly dancing, I realized this might be a class that would help me get in touch with my feminine side again, so I called the number on the flyer to get more information. A woman with a strong, distinct voice answered and explained to me the class was created to help women feel free in their bodies through dance. She added that the style of dance would leave me feeling strong, sexy, and confident. I was nervous, but I knew this was exactly what I needed. The class was being held during the exact time I was already scheduled to train my "sweaty money" client. So I had a decision to make: train the client who spent our entire session sexually harassing me or go take a class that would help me feel empowered. I realized as much as I needed the income, I had to take the class. I told my client that I would be unable to train him anymore. Predictably, he was very unhappy and told me, "Have fun learning how to be a stripper" and that he would be looking for me in the strip club — classy words from a married man.

Taking the dance class was one of the best decisions I ever made, and it offered much more than I had expected. The instructor had a unique method of teaching that forced us to look at and accept ourselves. She instructed the class to stand at the back of the room facing the mirror. Then she told us to walk towards our reflection while making eye contact with ourselves and staying fully engaged. This was very difficult for me because I felt ashamed of the person I saw in the mirror. I saw myself as the one who gave her power away to men and allowed men to abuse her verbally, emotionally, mentally and physically. These emotions often bubbled up to the surface while I danced, but it also helped me release them. During the class, we learned choreographed routines to beautiful, soulful music, but at the end, the instructor turned the lights off, and we had time to dance freely to a song she selected. This was my favorite part. I was able to move freely with no judgment, and I wanted more of this feeling. Eventually, I created my own version of the class to pass on the feeling of freedom and expression to other women.

My Spiritual Director was extremely pleased that I found a class like this and when I told her I wanted to create my own class, she thought it was a great idea. She suggested that I come up with a different name, one that didn't use the word "exotic" since the word had such a negative connotation to the general public. Not long after, while taking a run on my favorite Dallas trail, the name "Female Factor" came to me and would eventually evolve into my business name "Female Factor Fitness." Adding the word "fitness" was important to me because I felt it was the vehicle that got people in the door to experience what

I was offering. I was helping women become the best, empowered version of themselves through movement.

Not long after, I decided to fire all my male clients. Although I had no idea how I was going to supplement this lost income, I didn't feel scared or worried like I had in the past. I knew that I needed to do this for my overall health and longevity.

# CHAPTER 10

# The Dark Night of the Soul

"The dark night of the soul is a journey into
the light, a journey from your darkness into the
strength and hidden resources of your soul."

- Caroline Myss

I was excited about this change in direction in my business. It felt good to be able to completely focus on the needs of women with my business. My original reasons for becoming a personal trainer had evolved into something much bigger. It was a way to not only heal myself but to use my experience and knowledge to help my clients heal as well. A huge shift in all areas of my life had happened, and I could see the light at the end of my long, dark tunnel. Even my shift in energy was apparent to those around me. I didn't tell anyone I was seeing this woman who I called my Spiritual Director, but people kept asking if I had changed my diet or workout regimen because I looked different. I was healthier and glowed from within.

However, it's often the darkest before the dawn, and I had more hurdles to clear. My journey to empowerment was far from over. I have come to realize that when someone is making their way out of the darkness towards the life God intends for them, the forces of darkness — whether it be called Satan, evil, hell on Earth, or fear in the deep subconscious mind — seem to grow stronger to try and pull them back in.

Now I'm bringing it full circle and back to the beginning of my story; that cold night in December 2007 when I awoke freezing, naked and alone, trying to find my way out of the darkness, searching for a light and for answers. The evening before, the gym's annual Christmas party had been held at my boss's new house. He was extremely proud to show it off and was particularly excited to show us his shed behind the house that he had converted into his "man-cave." At that point in my life, I rarely drank because my Spiritual Director had taught me that alcohol disrupts the flow of healing energy and my goal was to heal. The party was rowdy, and everyone was drinking, but it didn't bother me. These were my friends and co-workers, and I felt safe.

But then there I was, waking up on a hard, frozen concrete floor. My clothes were gone, and all I saw was a sliver of light coming from what looked like a door. I made my way towards it and fumbling, found the doorknob and opened the door. I was instantly hit by a blast of cold air, but at least I had sunlight and could see where I was. I realized I was in the shed behind the house belonging to my boss. The same boss and owner of the gym, who had previously told me to "take one for the team" and sleep with my client.

My clothes were tossed all over the room, and there was vomit on the ground where I had apparently slept all night. I had only ever thrown up once from drinking and twice from a stomach bug. Obviously, something was very wrong, but I was frozen and focused on gathering and putting on my clothes. Making my way to the house, I went inside. There was a fire burning in the fireplace in the den, and I laid down in front of it and fell back to sleep. At some point, I woke up briefly to a woman covering me with a blanket. It was my boss's wife. She didn't say a word. Didn't she want to know where I came from? I fell back asleep and slept until I felt well enough to get up and drive home.

As I was heading for the door of the house to leave, my boss came out of his room and said, "Well, well, well…look at you, party animal. You were drunk last night. You made us all drinks and got us as drunk as you." It didn't make sense. First of all, I knew I wasn't drunk. Second of all, I didn't even know how to make drinks. Something wasn't right. What I did know was that this feeling was familiar, and I felt more than just hung-over. My brain was fuzzy, and my head was heavy. I had felt this way one other time in my life, and it was when I was drugged at the nightclub. I went home and tried to process it all, hoping I would remember what had happened.

The next day my boss called and asked me to meet him at the gym. It was a Sunday, and the gym was closed. I was scared, and my heart felt like it was beating out of my chest, but I agreed to meet him in hopes he would fill in the blanks for me. Once I got there, he was all smiles. He told me that I was, "so much fun last night." He said that I "let" him, and another trainer take turns having sex with me and that I "really enjoyed it." I felt sick. I knew it wasn't true. I would have never allowed that even in the darkest period of my life.

As if his admission wasn't enough, he came towards me, pinned me to the wall, kissed me forcefully and tried to reach between my legs. I pushed him away as hard as I could. I had watched him touch women inappropriately for years in front of me at the gym. They never said anything against it, and now it was my turn. He told me that he had watched me date so many men over the years and that he just had to "have a taste." I bolted for the door and left. Apparently, I still wasn't strong enough to stand up to a man, defend myself, or report the assault. I still had work to do. When I got to the car, I began to cry uncontrollably. Then I collected myself and called my Spiritual Director.

I made an appointment to see her the very next day. Monday couldn't come soon enough for me at that point.

The next day when I arrived at my appointment, I made the decision not to talk to my Spiritual Director about what happened because I had a fear of it getting out to my colleagues as well as disappointing her and undoing the work we had done. Whether that was the right decision or not, I didn't want to start over. Instead, I was ready to move forward and take my power back. I was ready to face God and my shadow self and bring back my true authentic self into the light. I had entered what the world-renowned medical intuitive, Caroline Myss, calls the "Dark Night of the Soul," which for me was longer than this one night. It was a period of time that had lasted for years. Soon after, the gym closed. It was a blessing in disguise, and the perfect time to find another job opportunity that would take me out of this darkness.

# CHAPTER 11

## Bait and Switch

"If we share our shame story with the wrong person, they can easily become one more piece of flying debris in an already dangerous storm."

- Brené Brown

The year was 2008. I was 34, and once again, I had convinced myself that I could start anew without carrying the heavy baggage from the past. I found a new gym home down the street that most of my existing clients agreed to try. The fitness business is always centered around what is best for the customer, so moving gyms was always tough. On my first week at this gym, one of the trainers showed up to work with a tiny, brown, shaky, four-pound, one-year-old baby chihuahua that he had found on the street in his neighborhood. He made a bee-line for me and asked me if I could give the dog a home. I said, "You are crazy, I can't take care of a dog." Not one minute later I had him in my arms, and my client encouraged me to take him. I didn't know the first thing about dogs and had decided long ago that I was not going to be one of those crazy dog ladies, but I named this adorable little bundle of fur "Pepe" and took him home.

My new pup went from scared and shaky to fiery and energetic. He began to take over my apartment, and I let him. Pepe had decided he wasn't going to tolerate it when a man came over. He was like a pit bull stuck in a chihuahua's body. Even Scott, a new guy I had met who had dogs of his own, didn't garner Pepe's approval. I started to realize that Pepe had a much better read on men than I did.

Scott chased me hard, determined to get a date with me. Finally, he wore me down, and when I agreed to a date, he rolled out the red-carpet treatment. He was charming, soulful, and deep. We would talk for hours about life and how we had common wounds from our past relationships. I told him everything — the good, the bad and the ugly. Things seemed to be going well until about a month into the relationship when I realized this was another "bait and switch." The charm and sweetness wore off, and a controlling, cold individual emerged. I began to see another man who was a narcissist and a gold medalist in extracurricular activities with women. I was now becoming my own gold medalist in catching these men when they lied. He would lash out in anger if I asked a simple question about where he had been or who he was with. He would turn it around on me and make me feel like I was the one who did something wrong when he was the one who was being unfaithful and projecting his guilt onto me. When I brought up to Scott that one of my girlfriends saw him out with another girl, he called her a "stupid bitch" and said that all my friends were not my friends and just jealous of our relationship. Scott would also make me feel like I was unattractive physically and incapable of pleasing him in the bedroom. The slightest things would turn him off when we were in the middle of sex, and then he would tell me what I needed to do or work on to please him, chipping away at my self-esteem little by little.

Though the abuse I experienced was only verbal and emotional, it still left deep scars. Scott used all he knew of my past pain and hurt against me, often calling me a slut and a whore. He made me believe that the past abuse I experienced was my fault, knowing I already beat myself up continuously. I was being victimized by a common technique used by narcissistic and controlling men. In the beginning, the man is extremely loving, supportive, giving and in-tune emotionally and spiritually, which makes the object of their attention feel alive and energized. Once they have established control and relationship buy-in from the woman, their energy shifts, the game changes and they become energy vampires, leaving her feeling drained and exhausted.

It took years to realize that all of these manipulation tactics were a form of "gaslighting," a term that came from the 1940's movie where a husband slowly manipulated his wife into thinking she was going crazy. Narcissists, like Scott and most of the men I attracted, used gas-lighting to keep me unsure of myself. Narcissists have a way of using their words in a cunning and manipulating way to convince you that *you* are the problem and that no one else would put up with being in a relationship with you. And whole-hearted individuals like me, always believe them.

One night after one of our many fights, I had another bizarre accident that shocked me back into reality. This time instead of a medicine ball being hurled at my face, it involved a pair of scissors. I was using a pair of scissors to open a makeup kit that was tightly wrapped in plastic, and after a few attempts, the scissors slipped and sliced into the middle of my left index finger. I froze in shock over what I had just done, and then came the pain and blood. I scrambled to find something to wrap my finger with and then decided to call Scott for help. Of course, he thought I was over-exaggerating the amount of pain I was in until he arrived and saw how deep the wound was. I ended up driving myself to the emergency room, and as I lay there, it hit me — yet another "I've been here before" lightbulb moment. There had to be some sort of connection to these accidents, my health issues, and the chaos that was always swirling around me. It was becoming clear to me that staying in these types of volatile and abusive relationships were causing me to attract more negativity into my life. This meant more than just physically staying away from these kinds of men; it involved cleaning up my energy so that I wouldn't even invite these men into my life. Still, it seemed I wasn't quite ready to move wholly to that new level.

I managed to stay with Scott for a while longer, dating off and on for a year. During this time, I had the biggest crush on an R&B superstar, and one of my girlfriends surprised me with a ticket to his concert at a popular venue in downtown Dallas. Scott was particularly jealous this time in our relationship and was not thrilled that I was going to the concert with my girlfriend, but I was excited that he wasn't going with us. Dressed in dark jeans, a gold strapless top, and gold heels I headed out for the evening. The concert venue was very intimate, so even though we were in the balcony section, I still felt like my star crush was singing directly to me, and I loved every minute of it. After the concert, my friend and I went into the lounge area to have drinks. We didn't realize the singer was in an enclosed tented area within the lounge, so when we saw a line was forming, I went to go see why. I realized it was a chance to meet my crush and my girlfriend urged me to go for it. I stood in the line for a few minutes, until suddenly the girl next to me said, "It's you!" I responded, "What's me?" She said, "He's picked you!"

The next thing I knew, I was pulled into a room by what appeared to be one of the star's bodyguards. He asked me to tell him something interesting about myself. I froze for a moment, then blurted out that I was a personal trainer as well as an identical twin. He seemed disappointed in my response but escorted me into the tent. The bodyguard asked me if I wanted to meet "him" and I excitedly responded, "Yes, of course!" He turned me around, and there was my crush standing in front of me wearing a casual button down and jeans. I was speechless. He stuck out his hand and the next thing I knew, we were racing out of the back of the tent, through a door, and into the main concert hall. At this point, I started to get nervous.

He and the bodyguard quickly led me down three flights of stairs. I guess I wasn't moving fast enough because the singer laughed and said, "Aren't you a personal trainer?" Of course with that, I picked up the pace, but I started to get even more anxious as we got closer to the bottom of the stairs and heard the loud sounds of the buses outside. When we got outside, the bodyguard looked at me and told me not to move because he had to put the star on the bus first. At this point, my anxiety turned to panic as I realized why we were there. I had been chosen as the "girl of the night." Yes, I had a crush on the artist and wanted to meet him, but I never dreamed I would be in this situation. After all, he was married. Surprise, surprise.

I looked down at my phone and saw that all my girlfriends, as well as Scott, were worried about where I was and had called my phone repeatedly. The bodyguard came back one more time and told me that there were still too many people around the bus and for me not to move, and then he went back to the bus. At that moment, I decided to turn and run. I ran all the way up the stairs in my heels and back into the concert hall. I tried every door I could find, even banging on every one of them, terrified I was going to get locked in there. Finally, the manager of the concert hall opened one of the doors. I said to him, "Can you believe I ran from a superstar? Who does that?" and he said, "A cool chick does. A chick I have respect for." That felt so good to hear. I felt so empowered. It was the first time I had gotten out of an uncomfortable and potentially dangerous situation with a man.

Scott, on the other hand, didn't speak to me the rest of the night, which was typical after I had done something he disapproved of. In this case, he couldn't get over that I was so close to getting on the bus. I decided that I couldn't be with Scott anymore. I think even Pepe was happy when I finally let him go. I cried for weeks. Pepe licked my tears. My energy shifted for the better.

# CHAPTER 12

# Rise Up

"Each time a woman stands up for herself,
she stands up for all women."

- Maya Angelou

One out of three women and girls on our planet — which equates to more than one billion women — will be sexually or physically abused in their lifetime. According to the Rape, Abuse, Incest, National Network (RAINN), 90% of rape and sexual assault victims are women. I truly believe that finding a group of people who have been through similar struggles can be an amazing catalyst to begin any healing process.

In January of 2013, I was tagged by a friend in a video online. The video showed a group of high school girls dancing to a beautiful song about breaking the chains of abuse. The lyrics and their dance really spoke to me. I realized that this was more than just an inspiring video floating around online. It was a call to action, an instructional video for a global dance flash mob that was created by Eve Ensler and her organization "One Billion Rising" to raise awareness of sexual abuse of women and girls all over the world. The event was scheduled to happen on Valentine's Day, which was less than a month away. The dance moves were choreographed by one of my dance idols, Debbie Allen, who also starred in one of my favorite movies as a child, *Fame*. I felt I had to be a part of this dance movement, and I connected with the woman who was leading the initiative in Dallas. I quickly became one of the lead dance instructors of our Dallas group. We held two practices each week right up until Valentine's Day, not only so they could learn the steps, but also to help the women express the feeling of dance in their bodies and spirit. This is the exact moment when I realized that my personal relationship with dance was more about healing.

The women who came to dance that day represented all ethnicities and backgrounds, many experiencing abuse as I had. These women instantly became my sisters, my family. Many of these women endured sexual abuse as a child by a parent or family member. I remember one young high school girl who shared her story of rape by a trusted caregiver and when she was in high school; she tried to take her life. Thankfully, she has found ways to cope and now writes poetry and shares her transformative journey by speaking at the event. Her story is just one of a billion others, and sadly not everyone is so lucky.

At the time, I felt there was a topic that still wasn't addressed, an important subject: the day-to-day sexual harassment and assault that is often endured by women in the professional arena and in everyday relationships of all kinds between men and women. I felt like these women needed a voice too. Fast forwarding to 2017; that voice spoke and was heard with the rise of the "Me Too" movement. It was way past due.

I continue to work with the One Billion Rising organization, but now I am different. After the "Victimhood" Stage and the "Validation" stage (which I will explain later), there comes a time when you experience anger. Up until this point, I had always believed that anger was unhealthy or not "Christian-like." Now I understand that anger is a necessary part of healing as long as we don't stay there but rather use it as a catalyst to move to the next level of our transformation. I had so much anger when I began my work with this group. Each year I participate, I let go of a little more anger, a little more shame that I had stored away for the men who hurt me. When we numb the pain, we numb the light, and we must understand that shame is lethal.

Part of my purpose in writing my story is to help those just beginning their healing journey. This means letting go of the anger, fear, and accusations and forgiving the men who inflicted the wounds in order to experience liberation and live victoriously.

# CHAPTER 13

# Fight, Flight, or Freeze and Why I Didn't Report

"You matter. What happened to you matters.
Your cases matter."

- Mariska Hargitay

After years of working with my Spiritual Director, I met another woman who also made a significant impact on my life. I will call her "SD2." Her general approach was in some ways very similar to my current one, but she had some distinctly different ones as well. Both women used God as their ultimate source, but my SD2 focused more on healing the past and reprogramming the brain. On my first appointment with her, she told me she saw that I would be doing a two or three-part video series for women. Oddly enough, shortly after that first visit, I was selected to choreograph and star in my first fitness DVD for Prevention Magazine. This was my big break!

Prevention Magazine is one of the largest and leading publications for women nationwide. If I could have bottled the energy I was emitting at that time in my life, I would have. I had an unshakable confidence, and I finally felt valuable. For the first time in my life, I got a taste of what I called "the flow," also known by many people as being "in the zone." When a person is engaged in an activity that gives them a sense of unwavering clarity, mastery, confidence, and joy that replaces the negative self-talk, fear, and hopelessness, a significant change in the brain takes place and flow happens.

As I began to embrace my new mindset and strength, I decided I had to dig deeper to understand why I didn't fight back or flee during an assault or report it afterwards. You as the reader might be wondering the exact same thing. Thinking back to my studies on the brain from my pharmaceutical sales rep days and conducting some additional research in neurobiology of trauma, I found some surprising information. The area of the brain called the pre-frontal cortex is the part that handles how a person will react when under an assault or attack. Typically serving as the executive decision-making center, this is the part of the brain that shuts off or goes offline when the body is in a dangerous, stressful, or traumatic situation and typical thinking and reasoning actions are incapacitated. In those situations, the "fear circuitry" in the brain takes over. At that point, our sympathetic nervous system, which oversees survival reflexes and self-protection, kicks into overdrive and reacts in one of three ways: fight, flight or freeze.

Looking back at the situations in my life where I felt threatened by a man physically, I tended to freeze. In my sessions with my Spiritual Directors, I explained that when I found myself in those types of situations, it felt like someone took over my body and I was unable to move, cry out, or think clearly. The technical term for this reaction or lack of reaction is called tonic immobility. A study published in *Acta Obstetrecia et Gynecologica Scandinavica* reports that out of nearly 300 women who visited the rape clinic, 70% experienced at least "significant" tonic immobility and 48% met the criteria for "extreme" tonic immobility during the rape. The conditions' severity was assessed using a scale that measured feelings of being frozen, mute and numb. As it turns out, most people, when put in a situation where their physical well-being feels threatened, will freeze versus fight or flee. For example, a person approaches you with a gun and demands your purse. Like most people, you would freeze to try to process what was happening and then hand over your purse. Very few people would fight back or try to get away unless they had specific military or police training and could overcome that initial instinct. This is especially true when it comes to assaults carried out by someone the victim knows. Knowing that this was a common reaction among assault victims and understanding what happened to me in those moments helped me let go of the shame I was holding on to. I finally stopped thinking that I deserved what happened in some way because I didn't fight them off or run.

After traumatic events such as sexual assault and rape, two other areas of the brain — the amygdala and the hippocampus — become overactive and go into overdrive, and they produce heightened emotions, stress, anxiety, and fear. This helped me understand why I never reported any of my assaults. Part of it was that I truly believed that this was normal behavior and that I had to stay in "pleaser mode" to keep them happy so they wouldn't hurt or leave me. The second part had to do with society's rush to blame the victim. According to the National Sexual Violence Resource Center, rape is the most under-reported crime with 63% of cases not reported to police, and the prevalence of false reporting is 2%. Most women don't report out of fear of being met with accusatory and judgmental questions such as "What were you wearing?" or "Are you sure it wasn't consensual?" I didn't scream and yell at any of my attackers. I didn't call the police or tell people close to me after an assault occurred because I was terrified of looking like damaged goods or being accused of making it up. Victims of sexual assault and abuse already wear a heavy armor of shame, guilt, and fear, and questions like those add more weight to the suffering because they insinuate that they, the victim, are the one to blame. Finally, I had clues as to what happened to me during and after an assault, and even years later in a consensual relationship when I got triggered by a past memory and shut down like I was being attacked all over again.

One Sunday, I turned on my TV and saw that a Law & Order SVU marathon was on. I happened to catch back-to-back episodes where Olivia Benson, played by Mariska Hargitay, was helping this young, smart, straight-laced college girl who had gone out to the same local bar on two separate occasions and was drugged and raped by a fellow college student. I broke out in tears watching as she tried to piece the night together and understand why it had happened to her twice. I could see and feel the fear and shame take over her body while Olivia explained the concept of "revictimization" to her. The risk of revictimization, according to the CDC, is based on vulnerability factors. One of these factors is the existence of PTSD, or Post-Traumatic Stress Disorder, in the victim from a previous assault. PTSD could give the victim the appearance of vulnerability in dangerous situations and affect their ability to defend themselves. It's rather mind-blowing for me to look back at my past and see how most men in my life shifted from sweet and charming to controlling and predatory. They even developed a look about them, and every single one of them had it. It was as if someone else inhabited their bodies, and they took on a disconnected emptiness and presence that was devoid of love, light, or compassion.

PTSD can also cause a victim to become hypersexual as a way to reassert a measure of control over their sexuality. I experienced both revictimization and hypersexuality throughout my victim stage. Sometimes the information we need comes to us from unexpected sources, and watching the SVU episodes gave me even more proof that I needed to change the energy I was broadcasting and reprogram my subconscious mind. I needed to move out of the victim state, establish strong personal boundaries, and start valuing and honoring myself. Unfortunately, I wasn't quite there yet, and life served up a few more hurdles and lessons for me to learn. The three final abusers — the Gym Manager, the Pastor, and the Producer — managed to cause deep wounds, but also the greatest shift in my quest for self-love and compassion.

# CHAPTER 14

# The Gym Manager, The Pastor, & The Producer

"Some women fear the fire, some women simply become it."

- Author Unknown

The Gym Manager

In the Spring of 2013, I had just finished my workout at the gym where I was training my clients at the time and decided to use the single person sauna in the women's locker room. I had been in there for about 15 minutes when my manager walked into the locker room and opened the sauna door. I still had a towel wrapped around me, but unfazed he exclaimed, "Let me see!" I stood there in complete shock. Just like before, I couldn't move or speak. He grabbed for my towel, again saying, "Let me see!" It happened so fast I didn't have time to react or stop him. There I was, defenseless and standing there completely naked in front of him. Suddenly something new happened, a reaction I had never had before. I began to cry. Looking back, I think I cried because I was so tired of it all, exhausted from men preying upon me and from not being able to do anything about it. Thankfully, it was all it took. My reaction must have scared him, and he ran out of the locker room. I had won, and this time the perpetrator fled. I had to find a way to get out of that gym immediately. I could no longer work for him.

The Pastor

It was August of 2015, and I decided I needed to get back to listening to God and find a church community. Getting asked out by a pastor of a church seemed like it was the perfect sign from God. I felt like I was finally attracting the kind of man who would respect me and treat me well. He was very charming and asked me to accompany him to church for our first date. It couldn't get any safer than that I thought, and I excitedly picked out a dress to wear. It had been a long time since I had been asked out on a proper date.

The pastor showed up to pick me up an hour before church services began. As I saw him get out of his car, I got hit with an overwhelming feeling that I had been here before. Later I realized that this feeling was not butterflies, but rather a gut feeling that was telling me to get the hell out of there. At the time, I didn't pay attention and ignored it. He was nice looking and incredibly likable. The church was amazing. We had a front row seat to the incredible music and sermon. Oddly, I got another sign that something might not be right. This time it was more than just a feeling, it was a physical tap on the shoulder. The woman sitting next to me tapped me on the shoulder and said that she liked what I had done to my hair, that I looked good blonde. I was confused, but I mentally pushed it off and enjoyed the service.

After the church services were over, he took me on an elaborate all-day date beginning with brunch, then from there to a dessert bar with wine and expensive chocolates. He had an Ed Sheeran song keyed up on his phone for us to slow dance to and I fell hook, line, and sinker. I felt so comfortable with him that I began to share some stories of my past. After all, he was a pastor with a ministry that claimed to help people learn how to forgive and let go of the pain. He had also written several books, including one about why people shouldn't have premarital sex. I felt relaxed, comfortable and happy that I had found a man who was interested in more than just sex. At the end of the date, he politely walked me to my door, gave me a big hug and asked me for another date. We decided on the following weekend, and he went home.

Less than 24 hours later, the third warning indicator light came on. He apparently didn't plan on waiting for a whole week until our next date. After a day full of texting back and forth with him, he called me and told me to look out my window. Again, that terrible gut feeling wrenched through me. I went over to the window, and there he was, standing in what looked like gym attire. I had just gotten off work and wasn't in the mood to see anyone. He said, "Well, aren't you going to let me in?" and he raised up a bag. "I made you dinner."

This was too much for me at that point, but I let him in anyway. He was adamant that we eat right away, but then scolded me in a rather aggressive tone when I took a bite before he could say grace. We finished dinner and moved to my couch to relax and talk. My "guard dog" Pepe showed his disapproval as he growled, bared his teeth and moved closer to me. I started to feel like his intentions were more than just dinner as he inched closer to me on the couch and then grabbed my feet so he could give me a foot massage. I was feeling increasingly uncomfortable, and I pulled my foot away. I wanted to get to know him more, and I wanted to know his thoughts about what I shared the day before. I wanted his perspective as a pastor and pushed him for his input. He said that he understood that I had "issues" with sex and that he was okay with that. He also emphasized that *he* didn't have any problems with sex. I asked, "So you don't believe in premarital sex, right?" to which he answered, "Well its complicated" and went on to say that since he didn't have a problem with sex like I did, that he could handle having sex before marriage. What a hypocrite! I was completely turned off. He had written a book on why the Bible says premarital sex is wrong and yet obviously didn't live by his own preaching. I didn't bother calling him out on it. I was done and ready for him to go home.

He didn't even give me a chance to get up from the couch. He came towards me with so much strength, and I couldn't stop him. I told him to stop and said "NO!" several times, but nothing worked. I felt myself float up and out of my body to my safe place until it was over. Afterward, he got up immediately to collect himself and leave, and I started to cry. He said, "Maybe you should put on some music that would make you happy" and then he left. Pepe licked my tears again. I never heard from him again.

Devastated, I didn't get out of bed for an entire day. I was in too much emotional pain and wanted to die. I wanted to report him to the church; I wanted him to pay for what he had done, but I was still too weak. I backtracked his social media accounts to see if there were clues, and the only thing I really found was an ex-girlfriend who was around my age, a personal trainer, with dark hair. A girlfriend that he had taken to the same places he took me on our first date. That explained the woman's comment to me at church.

Here I was — not only had it happened again, but this time the predator was someone who I thought was a good man, one that believed in the same God that I did. At that point, I lost all hope that I was ever going to find a man who would respect me. I also had to face the hard fact that I had not fully healed. I was still putting out an energy that predators picked up on. This is proof that you can have all the best intentions in the world, but if you don't put them into practice and live that energy day in and day out, then you will get the same result. I think this may also be the definition of insanity.

The Producer

Months later, I met the third and final predator, a local producer. After meeting this man one time, I felt like he genuinely believed in my brand and my vision to help women. He told me that he was filming a fitness reality TV show and I was a perfect fit. I should have realized this was too good to be true. He asked me to meet him at his studio for a one-on-one collaboration meeting to go over his project, to look at my work and show me around the studio. My schedule was hectic at the time, so my availability was limited, but I agreed to meet him the following week after my workday ended. Looking back, I should have never met him alone at his studio after hours, but I believed that he really thought I had talent, and I felt safe because we had mutual friends. He gave me a tour of the studio and then led me upstairs to see the video/movie viewing room. That's when the terrible gut feeling came back and started to overcome me as we went up the spiral staircase. Once we were upstairs, he told me to dance for him because he needed to see what "I had." I stood there, frozen and then he repeated the request. For the first time in my life, I couldn't dance. I should have left that very second. Why didn't I run?

He pulled down his pants and told me to come over and give him a blow job. Of all the terrible, sick, twisted stories of my past, this one is the most difficult to tell, because after everything I had been through and all the lessons I thought I had learned, I still did what he told me to do. Why did I not tell him he was a disgusting pig? Did I loathe myself that much? Sadly, the answer was YES. I loathed myself that much. Afterward, he zipped up his pants and told me I was "fun" and that he needed to get up early for work and walked me to the door of the studio. I barely made it to my car before the tears started to stream down my face. The frightened little girl inside me was exhausted. She had endured too much, and this was her rock bottom. It was time for her to face her fears, heal her past wounds, and rise like a phoenix. The ascent had begun.

# THE VULNERABILITY

# CHAPTER 15

# My Millennial Meltdown

"You can't get to courage without
walking through vulnerability."

- Brené Brown

Every experience gives you the opportunity to grow. What I like to refer to as my "millennial meltdown" began on January 1st, 2017. What started as an attempt at a fun, casual fling with a younger man became an opportunity for me to learn some of the most valuable lessons I had learned to date and the catalyst for the final phase of my transformation. I thought dating a man 20 years younger would give me a sense of vindication, a way to take my power back from the older men who hurt me in my past.

Everyone around me assumed the relationship was just the typical cougar-younger man fling, but nothing could have been further from the truth. This young man was as eccentric and quirky as me, and he brought out my inner child. It felt good to live in the moment. I felt free, free to be my true authentic self. It was becoming clear that we were in each other's lives for a reason; to teach each other something that we both needed to learn in our own lives. When we met, I still needed to work through the final stages of my anger and forgive the men who hurt me in order to move forward. I realized this would require me to tap into my feminine side, the side of me I pushed far back into the shadows of my soul.

It's very difficult to live in the present when you know that you both are ultimately going in different directions, and I knew our relationship was on a timer. I found myself adopting "millennial behaviors," even agreeing to announce our relationship status on social media. It felt good to show the world that I was dating a man half my age. I saw older men flaunting their relationships with younger women all the time, so if they could do it and be praised, why couldn't I? At this point, however, I started to realize that I was staying in the relationship for the wrong reasons and my ego was calling the shots. Not a day would go by without a woman asking me how I could date a man so much younger. They told me they would feel too insecure about their physical appearance as the older woman. The odd thing was, for the first time in my life, I didn't feel insecure about my physical appearance because I knew I looked better than I did in my 20's; however, I did have some insecurities when it came to my professional life. I was watching this 23-year-old, with so much energy and focus, actively building a foundation for himself and accomplish things in the fitness industry that had taken me years to achieve and even some I was still trying to master. I got caught up in supporting and encouraging him to leave his traditional 9 to 5 corporate job to pursue his online business. Eventually, I realized I was helping him at the expense of myself. And I was ignoring what I had to do to accomplish my own goals in life.

It was time to take care of my own shit. After about two months of living moment by moment and broadcasting every moment of our relationship on social media, reality started to really set in. I started thinking seriously about my future, personally and professionally, from a realistic perspective as a single woman in her 40's. My inner critic was constantly telling me that I was worthless and sad because here I was at 43, having worked my butt off for 20 years with nothing tangible to show for it. Although I had a young man interested in me and boosting my ego, I started to feel like I was washed up and old news when it came to my business. I started getting emotional and would cry for no reason. It crossed my mind that I might be going through early menopause. I became convinced something was wrong with my hormones, so I sought out one of the top functional medicine doctors in Dallas to run the labs

I needed. Thankfully as it turned out, I wasn't in menopause; rather, I was going through my first life crisis as I referred to earlier as "the dark night of the soul."

For me, that night was a succession of nights strung together over many years. You might recognize this in your own life as the moment when you stop and realize you have been grinding and hustling your entire life — whether it's raising kids and being a wife, or like me, putting every ounce of energy into your dream and vision. You may have forgotten to make time to date or have a personal life because you were so determined to have your dream come to life. It's very difficult, regardless of which scenario is yours, to come that far in your life and realize that you might have to change course, create something new, or alter your dream. I knew I wasn't happy working hour to hour in the fitness industry. I also realized another timer was ticking. Teaching class was strenuous and hard on me physically, and it was time to start thinking about what was next. I didn't know what that next step should be. After all, I had been on autopilot for years and didn't have a sustainable plan in place.

Not knowing what the next step in life looks like is one of the most difficult struggles we face. When women reach this pinnacle, often beginning in their early 40's, it is often categorized as a mid-life crisis, the results of menopause, or even a breakdown. I had the gift of helping other people find their next big project or idea, but I couldn't do it for myself. I had so many excuses. I compared myself to my young boyfriend and decided that I had more stress, more baggage, bills to pay, higher insurance, more responsibility, and more to lose. Although they were valid concerns, they were also the excuses I was loading my argument with that allowed me to hold back from taking real action. I was so tired of being on the hamster wheel and decided to do something about it. I started brainstorming about creating programs for women that would help them not only physically, but mentally and emotionally as well. I finally felt I was gaining some momentum, but I also realized I was ready for more in my life than just work.

As I worked on my new programs, my realization and understanding of the holistic approach to health and happiness deepened. It became increasingly clear that a person can have all the support and tools at their fingertips, but they are the ones who must act if they want to change. They can decide to stay where they are, convincing themselves it's safer and more comfortable or that they are too old to start something new. They can even keep themselves busy with things that distract them. Fear manifests itself in many ways, causing people to become bitter and depressed. In order to overcome that fear, they must lean into their discomfort, allow themselves to become vulnerable, and in the process, they will discover their authentic selves. This was the message I felt I not only needed to share with the women around me but also one I needed to teach myself.

I realized that this young man and I were drifting further apart and the differences in our life stages were becoming more apparent by the day. As much as we both wanted to believe that he was already a full-grown man at 23 years old, the truth was that he hadn't truly lived yet. To make it worse, I felt like I was sacrificing myself and my dreams to provide a foundation for him.

It was time for me to act like an adult and end the relationship. Knowing that relationships like these often continue on a limited basis out of convenience, we made a clean break. Our relationship had given me the perspective I needed to let go of all the anger I was still holding on to towards the men in my past. I had taught him how to open his heart and love, and he opened my eyes to the fact that I was far from done. I knew it was time to forgive the past and time to look forward and return to love. I focused on myself and fell deeper in love with who I was on the inside.

# THE VICTORY

# CHAPTER 16

# The Victory Dance

"Be strong when you are weak, brave when
you are scared, and be a beacon of hope
for others when you are **victorious**."

- Victoria Griffith

When we regain what we lost, we see it on a deeper level. I started out in this world as an innocent, bright-eyed, confident young girl who was ready to take on the world. I believed if I followed the rules that I learned in Bible studies and church, I would stay perfect and safe like the bubble I grew up in. If I could go back in time and talk to my younger self, I would tell her that there is no such thing as "perfect" and falling down is a part of growing up. It is in the falling where we learn what it means to have faith. Faith that it will always work out if we listen to our inner voice, inner guidance, our divine source. Whether you call this source God, Creator, a Higher Power, or the Universe, I believe we all have access to this constant flow of divine data. Richard Rohr, Franciscan priest and founder of the Center of Action and Contemplation explains this so beautifully when he says, "God is not *out there*." Instead of looking outside of ourselves for the answers, we need to realize we have all the answers we need within ourselves.

I believe we create our own hell on earth when we choose to ignore this guidance system and follow our own twisted path. Unfortunately, that path often takes us away from the light and our own truth, into the darkness where we experience fear, physical and emotional disease (dis-ease), and a need for approval from others. Through my own struggles, I have discovered how we can live a victorious life here and now by transforming our suffering and experiencing our own personal resurrection from the inside out. Some people choose physical rituals to prove their transformation. Others, like me, experience a shift in consciousness — invisible to the naked eye — that can happen in an instant or over a period of years. Either way, you can't go back. This is the point when your life will begin again. You no longer have to feel unworthy, struggle with the need to be perfect, or settle for a life that is not allowing you to be the best version of your true authentic self. It's time to begin to offer a new and improved energy to the world and realize you are in the driver's seat.

Today, at 44 years young, I look and feel better than I did in my 20's and 30's. In contrast to my initial timeline and plan, I am not married, and I don't have children. Things happened, and I was forced to face the fact that I had to write a very different fairytale ending for myself; one that doesn't necessarily end with a husband, two kids and a house with a two-car garage. Some might see this as the ultimate failure, others might see it as the ultimate freedom. As women, we have a tendency to rush into a marriage, begin living for our partners and having babies while completely neglecting our own sacred contracts and dreams. There are also many women who have never felt the urge to have children. There is no one single answer for anyone. Listening to your true authentic self and making choices based on what you want from your life as opposed to what society tells you that you are supposed to do, is the key. Whether you choose to be married or single, and to have children or not, to be truly happy with any choice you make, you must fall in love with yourself first.

After years of searching for love in all the wrong places, I had found the love I was avoiding my entire life. A love so strong that it washed away the feelings that I was damaged goods or that I was not enough. A love that allowed me to appreciate my body without starving or beating it up through working out and recognize that I was sacred, valuable, and more than an object to be given to a man. Today, I am no longer a victim, nor am I defined by my past. I have traded the "V" for victim for the "V" of victory. Not only have I found my voice, but I have also found that I can truly love myself — body, mind, and soul. I now dance with newfound freedom and conviction. This is my victory dance.

# CHAPTER 17

# Ok, So Now What?

"She began to breathe again and soon found she
was in love. Not in love with anyone in particular,
but in love with her life. And for the first time,
in a long time, everything was exhilarating."

- Author Unknown

The most difficult part of any transformation is creating a lasting change. When you finally decide to make this shift out of the old and into the new, it can be truly intoxicating. Your brain and body are flooded with happy neurochemicals (more on that later). But what goes up must come down, and when you come down from this elated state of new bliss, it feels like you've taken two steps back. That is the precise moment I realized that I didn't need another diet or workout plan, I needed much more. I needed a CliffsNotes version of my own story, outlining the techniques I used to reach my personal victory so that I could refer to it when I felt like falling back into my old patterns of self-loathing, self-sabotage, and fear. It was similar to a diet plan that I would give my clients to keep weight off, but this plan would be the internal workout used to permanently silence the inner critic who bullied me into thinking I wasn't good enough. At this point, I was more than ready to release the mental and emotional weight that I had been carrying around for 25 years. And just as the goddess Victoria carries her wreath and sash to crown a victor, I want to inspire other women to do the same.

Trust me, I am not standing on a shiny pedestal saying that I have it all figured out. My transformation didn't happen in one night or even one year; it took decades. Even as I began writing this book, I realized that I had more pain to let go of and more wounds to heal. So now I want to help you make this shift without all the speed bumps I encountered on my journey.

Just as every physical body is different, everybody's individual emotional journey is different, and there is no one-size-fits-all, cookie-cutter plan for learning how to love yourself and experience true happiness. We must align our heads with our hearts and figure out what true happiness looks like for us while addressing our whole selves physically, mentally, and spiritually. On the next few pages, I share the "Five V's" that allowed me to silence my inner critic, release my inner cheerleader, fall madly in love with myself and live a victorious life.

Before introducing you to these five techniques, I want you to visualize with me for a moment: think of your hand with its five fingers. The center of your hand represents your best life with each finger representing the stages we go through as victims. Your fingers, or energy circuits, can be opened or closed, broken or bent, but they are a necessary part of the whole as we heal and live victoriously.

The "Five V's"

Love notes to yourself

# THE FIVE V's

## Lesson 1: VICTIMHOOD

To take the first step towards loving myself, I had to ditch the victim mentality and remove the invisible scarlet letter I was wearing. When people used to tell me to stop feeling sorry for myself and learn to love myself, I almost felt like punching them in the face. Ok, not really, but you can't go straight from loathing yourself to loving yourself overnight. The inner critic in our head keeps us immobilized by fear and keeps us in the role of the victim. It is easier to stay attached to our victim story than to let it go because we've been telling this story for so long. We have created friendships, a life, and a mentality around our status as a victim.

Many people get stuck in a negative default mode that perpetuates throughout their life, due to old thought patterns that began in childhood. Since these thoughts are buried deep in the subconscious mind, it requires rewiring the neural pathways (the brain's circuits) through a process called neuroplasticity in order to make a real change in direction. Neural pathways are like train tracks that run throughout the brain. We have the choice to keep those thought trains stuck on the same negative tracks with the stories we continue to tell ourselves, or we can make a move to relocate our thought trains onto new positive thought tracks and create new stories.

Scientists say we have fifty to seventy thousand thoughts a day, and ninety percent of those are the ones we had yesterday. This is crucial information because our ability to heal is directly affected by negative thoughts, which in turn weaken the immune system. If most of a person's thought patterns are negative and they stay in that mindset, it creates the perfect environment for illness and disease in the body. I personally chose not to allow a medical diagnosis to define or label me, as this can also block healing. Follow my 4 steps below to jump on a positive track, and catch the next train out of victimhood and on to bigger and better things.

Practice: Steps to retrain your brain

1. Catch the negative thoughts immediately: "We aren't going down that track today."

2. Slow that negative thought train down and throw the fearful cargo off the train.

3. Find something positive to focus on that you are grateful for, an "attitude of gratitude."

4. Reassure yourself that you are free from any label
   — medical diagnosis labels or negative judgment
   (including the self-imposed "V").

## Lesson 2: VALIDATION

Perfectionism isn't possible, but transformation is. Once you let go of self-imposed timelines, comparing yourself to others, and accepting your body, you will begin loving who you see in the mirror. I grew up in an environment where everyone seemed "perfect" on the outside, so the stage was set for disappointment early on. From a very young age, I dreamed of going to college, getting married, and raising kids, just like everyone else in the community I grew up in. When that didn't happen on my timeline, I began to feel like I wasn't good enough or that something was wrong with me, and I channeled the need to be perfect into my job and achievement addiction. I had to be the best teacher, the best trainer, in the best shape, and the list goes on. I confused being busy with being successful. The more I tried to be perfect, the more miserable I became. At every turn, I ended up on the negative track back to victimhood. I had to learn how to accept that I was enough, that I was exactly where I needed to be, and that I needed to enjoy the process of living without comparing myself to those around me. Back in my 20's, I thought I wanted marriage/kids/etc.; but once I discovered my true authentic self, I realized that I was working harder to please my family and friends rather than trying to please myself. Whether your desire is to find the partner of your dreams or follow your dreams to discover your purpose in life (or both), you must first enjoy the process of living outside of your plan. Trade in your rigid "to-do list" for a flexible "in the now" list. Begin thinking in terms of changing your life based on energy vibration versus a rigid timeline.

You are one-of-a-kind. You must accept and fall in love with the unique body you are given. In my quest for the "perfect" body, I spent years beating my body up and jumping from one fad diet to the next. In my health and wellness practice, I work with so many women who want me to give them a cookie-cutter, quick fix, one-size-fits-all plan to help them lose the physical weight. There is no one-size-fits-all when it comes to beauty. Everyone has different nutritional and workout needs. Stop comparing yourself to others, accept your unique size and shape, and create attainable life goals; not just the short term, "I want to wear a bikini by summer" goals. When you have actionable self-love rituals like the ones I've outlined below, it's amazing how much easier it is to look and feel your best. Falling in love with your unique body, mind, and soul is the key to lasting health and wellness.

Practice: Self-love rituals to add to your daily routine

1.  Journal

    Set aside at least 10 minutes a day for journaling. Creating time to do this forced me to look inward, helped me complete my healing journey, and gave me the courage to write this book. Begin by journaling one thing you are grateful for. Start with a physical trait and then move into other areas of your life. Watch how much easier it becomes once you start.

2.  Mirror Work

    When you wake every morning and before bed at night, look at yourself in a mirror and say, "I love you. You are enough." It may feel silly, but remember you are trying to lay down new positive thought tracks in your brain. Personally, I even write myself a love note on a sticky or with markers on the mirror.

3.  Eat and workout right for your unique body type

    Since there is no one-size-fits-all plan for workouts or nutrition, I recommend taking the Metabolic Typing Test. This test tells you the exact foods that are ideal for your metabolic and body type. This information can help create a customized workout and nutrition plan so that when you attain your goals, your outside will match your inside.

## Lesson 3: VOICE

Loving yourself requires discovering your inner victorious voice and taking your power back. I spent years living in silence and shame after my assaults because I was too afraid to speak up. I was too afraid that I would not be believed. Also, most of the women I know who are stuck in the cycle of abuse — like I was — are pleasers by nature and are unable to utter the word "No." By not setting strong boundaries, we give our power away. We must learn how to set healthy boundaries and only share our personal lives with those who earn our trust. This includes establishing boundaries for both your heart and your vagina. Your body is sacred, and you must truly treat it like a temple inside and out. When you stick to these healthy boundaries, you broadcast a new powerful, confident energy that literally breaks the cycle of becoming a victim again.

As we step into our power, we must also learn how to forgive ourselves as well as others. The wounds inflicted on you are not your fault, but your healing is your responsibility. Forgiving ourselves releases us from the shame and guilt we carry around as victims and is crucial in the healing process. As I explained in chapter 13, we must understand that we all react differently in threatening situations, so blaming ourselves for how we react in a stressful or dangerous situation is pointless. Part of forgiving ourselves is loving our dark parts. When we give love to our darkness, we elevate our vibration.

Forgiving those who inflict pain or harm is just as important. I have forgiven every single one of the men mentioned in my book who caused me pain. Forgiving the men who hurt me was tough, but I wasn't forgiving them for them. I forgave them for myself, so I could fully heal. Forgiveness is never about the other person. It is about taking your power back and putting an end to the pattern of abuse. When I forgave them, it was like I had taken off the ten-pound vest I had been wearing around for years. I began to see that these men were just as disconnected from their divine source as I was at the time. Now that I am healed, I can look back and mentally thank them for helping me discover who I truly am and for helping me find my voice so that I could share my story with other women.

Learning how to tune out the outside voices so that you can get to know yourself, even the not-so-pretty parts, is key to finding your voice. I obviously had difficulty with this step because I bounced from toxic relationship to toxic relationship without taking any time to be alone with myself, until my

Spiritual Director introduced me to meditation. Many people may think that meditation is woo-woo mumbo-jumbo only for devout Yogis. This couldn't be further from the truth. You can't get it wrong. Think of meditation as a deeper form of prayer and contemplation. I began by carving out 10 minutes in the middle of the day to meditate, whether I was sitting in my car or in a quiet space at work. The most difficult part was quieting my mind of the racing thoughts and items on my mental "to-do list." Just like my workouts, the more I practiced, the easier it became. Oh, and the added bonus? Your stress hormones will decrease while your anti-aging hormones increase.

Practice: Meditation to balance the heart and the head

1. Bring hands to heart center with fingertips touching your body (because our awareness moves to where our physical touch is).

2. Breathe in for 4 seconds, hold for 4 seconds, breathe out for 4 seconds, hold for 4 seconds

3. Feel gratitude in your heart to silence the judgment (inner critic) in your head.

## Lesson 4: VULNERABILITY

If you want to achieve balance in your body and harmony in your life, you must bring your head and heart into alignment. This requires just the right amount of vulnerability. Being vulnerable is a balancing act, and you must prepare to get comfortable with being uncomfortable. Each one of us has a masculine and feminine side that has less to do with gender and more to do with energy. During my journey, I bounced from living solely in my feminine energy in my younger years, to living on the other end of the energy continuum in my masculine energy. In both extremes, I was wearing a mask that prevented me from discovering my true authentic, balanced self. Often times, we suppress either our masculine or our feminine side. It is our job to work on finding the balance between both the masculine and the feminine, the head, and the heart.

I have seen a trend in our society lately where women are almost forced into living in their masculine. I feel this is a result of women feeling like they must do it all and do it all well. The new superwoman raises the kids, takes care of her husband, cooks, cleans, and holds down a full-time job outside of the home. The masculine side is associated with the *Ego* — the warrior and protector archetype — that operates from the head. This side is typically very competitive and can be controlling and rigid. Women who have a very strong masculine side are the women who have a more difficult time being vulnerable. They often have an easier time keeping boundaries and a harder time with forgiveness and letting other people in. The masculine side often emerges after a sexual assault, or as I described earlier, an assault on the divine feminine. I had an aversion to wearing anything girly and would make fun of women that were "girly-girls." I was trying to act like a man to protect myself from getting hurt by a man. This just caused me more pain because I was hiding who I really was on the inside. I needed to rescue the sacred feminine inside me. If this is you, learning how to get in touch with your feminine side allows you to soften those edges a bit and open your heart just enough so your true authentic self shines through and a more balanced woman emerges.

One of the activities that helped me heal my divine feminine was dance. I took all types of girly dance classes with poles, chairs, high heels, and other props and then I began teaching them. I realized that I didn't need any physical props or clothes to make me feel sexy because, for the first time in my life, I felt sexy on the inside. I still find dancing as one of the best ways to tap into the divine feminine because you are forced to let go of the rules in your head, relinquish control, and allow your heart to open.

There are many women with a more dominant feminine energy like I had in my younger years. The feminine side is your inner, sacred, intuitive self which operates from the heart. Women often are born wearing their hearts on the outside and being vulnerable comes naturally to us. Brené Brown calls this "whole-hearted." When your feminine energy is dominant, you are more in-tune with your sensitive, intuitive, healing side. Unfortunately, that can also mean you may be less in touch with how to establish boundaries that prevent you from being taken advantage of. Living from the heart alone can render you too vulnerable. This is why I felt so drained in my relationships with men. I allowed every single man in too easily because I didn't have strong boundaries or self-respect. If this is you, learning how to tap into your masculine energy will allow you to establish the boundaries needed to achieve a balance between the head and the heart. One great way that I recommend getting in touch with your masculine energy through movement is boxing because it will leave you feeling strong and empowered both physically and spiritually.

Practice: Movement Activities

> Choose one physical activity to try from the "Divine Feminine" and one activity from the "Divine Masculine" Movement groups below:

Divine Feminine Movement

These movements are typically fluid and intuitive with less structure or rules.

- Dance

- Yoga (Yoga can be both masculine and feminine, but because the act of slowing down and focusing on breath and the internal world is typically considered more of a feminine energy, I included it as a Divine Feminine Movement. Therefore, I suggest beginning with Restorative Yoga.)

- Body Weight Flow

- Water-based movement

Divine Masculine Movement

These movements are typically more powerful and strong with specific instruction for execution.

- Boxing

- Power Lifting

- Kettle Bell Work

- Weighted Bat Work

## Lesson 5: VICTORY – Finding your Flow

After using the typical clinical health and fitness assessment for 20 years with my clients, I realized that I needed a new approach. I traded the tape measure and the body fat calipers for a three-word question, "What moves you?"

The answer to that question, unique to each person, is what I touched on in Chapter 13 and what I like to call the "sweet spot" of life. This is a place where you feel your greatest sense of freedom, power, healing, and connection with your true authentic self, which results in your inner critic/saboteur taking a backseat. Think for a minute: What activity causes you to lose track of time and space, and you feel you are your best self? Mine is when I dance. I can get lost working on choreography for hours. I had no idea what was happening. I just knew that during those times, I traded in my external stressors and anxiety for a feeling of heightened clarity and natural energy. After doing my own extensive research on how the brain works in relation to stress and trauma and how to reverse those effects of them, I have now come to understand that this is what many scientists have named the "flow state" or most commonly referred to as getting into the "zone." The zone is the state of complete immersion in an activity where the *Ego*, our inner critic, disappears and you are living in the present moment, "the now," causing time to fly by.

Finding your flow state is particularly helpful in the healing process for those who deal with anxiety, depression, and addiction and are constantly seeking food, drugs, alcohol, or sex to self-soothe in some other manner. When in this state of flow, the brain naturally releases powerful neurochemicals — dopamine, serotonin, endorphin, oxytocin — that are meant to help boost mood and mentality. Dr. Mihaly Csikszentmihalyi, Ph.D., a pioneer researcher on flow state, believes that when a person is in the flow, they are able to tap into an endless supply of intrinsic motivation and creativity and that achieving a flow state on a regular basis is a key component of happiness.

Practice: Finding your Flow

Now let's work on finding your flow state. Think about what brings you the most joy that you do every day or as the younger version of you. If you can't think of anything right off the bat, then it's time for you to become a student. Try a class in art, dancing, or maybe cooking; try out anything that interests you and take the time to fully immerse yourself in it. If you can allow yourself to feel the flow of happiness, confidence, abundance, and freedom, then you are more likely to find ways to experience it on regular basis, ultimately leading you to a life with more meaning and purpose. I would love to see this as a part of every workout and nutrition program, ultimately connecting the mind, body, and soul.

Victorious

Finally, I want to thank you, the reader, for taking the time to pick up this book and giving me this opportunity to share with you my journey, my message, and my voice. I hope you find my "Five V's" helpful as you embark on this new relationship with your true divine self. Remember this is your journey. We spend so much of our time looking outside of ourselves for the answers, for love and acceptance, when everything we need is right here inside each one of us. Once you realize that you already are everything you are looking for, then you will be happier, you will be fulfilled, and you will *be victorious.*